MAHATMA GANDHI

MAHATMA GANDHI

HIS LIFE, WRITINGS AND SPEECHES

SAROJINI NAIDU

GYAN

Published by

Gyan Publishing House
5, Ansari Road
Daryaganj, New Delhi-110002
Phone: 011-47034999, 9811692060
E-mail: books@gyanbooks.com

Distribution Network
gyanbooks.com
India, USA, Canada, UK, Australia

ISBN: 978-93-7014-616-7 (HB)

First Published, 1917

2nd Impression 2025

Printed at: Gyan Press, Delhi.

MAHATMA GANDHI: HIS LIFE, WRITINGS AND SPEECHES
Author: SAROJINI NAIDU

Mahatma Gandhi—1917.

MAHATMA GANDHI

HIS LIFE, WRITINGS AND SPEECHES

WITH FOREWORD

BY

MRS. SAROJINI NAIDU

GANESH & CO., MADRAS

"I see in Mr. Gandhi the patient sufferer for the cause of righteousness and mercy, a truer representative of the Crucified Saviour than the men who have thrown him into prison and yet call themselves by the name of Christ."—*Lord Bishop of Madras.*

THE CAMBRIDGE PRESS, MADRAS

PUBLISHERS' NOTE

THE publishers feel that no apology or justification on their part is needed for sending out this volume to the public. All who honour nobility of purpose and high rectitude of conduct, all who honour Mr. Gandhi, who is as an embodiment of them, will be glad to have in a collected form the writings and speeches of a man whose words still linger behind his deeds. This volume is by no means exhaustive. Mr. Gandhi's speeches and writings lie scattered in various places and the task of collection is not yet over. When sufficient material has accumulated the Publishers hope to issue a second volume.

In conclusion, the Publishers desire to express their thanks to a friend of theirs who is responsible for the life-sketch, and to Mrs. Sarojini Naidu for having contributed the beautiful foreword found at the beginning of this volume.

CONTENTS

APPENDIX IV

APPENDIX V

APPENDIX VI

LIST OF ILLUSTRATIONS

FOREWORD

"It is only India that knows how to honour greatness in rags" said a friend to me one day as we watched Mahatma Gandhi cleaving his way through the surging enthusiasm of a vast assembly at Lucknow last year.

For, surely the sudden appearance of Saint Francis of Assisi in his tattered robe in the fashionable purlieus of London or Milan, Paris or Petrograd to-day were scarcely more disconcerting or incongruous than the presence of this strange man with his bare feet and coarse garments, his tranquil eyes, and calm, kind smile that disclaims even while it acknowledges a homage that emperors cannot buy.

But India, though she shift and enlarge her circumference age after age keeps true to her spiritual centre and retains her spiritual vision undimmed and eager to acclaim her saints. Let us not follow the conventional mode of the world and wait for a man to be dead to canonise him; but rather let our critical judgment confirm the unerring instinct of the people that recognizes in Mahatma Gandhi a lineal descendant of those great sons of compassion who became the servants of humanity—Gautama Buddha, Chaitanya, Ramanuja, Ramakrishna.

He lacks, may be, the breadth and height and ecstacy of their mystical attainment: but he is not less than theirs in his intensity of love, his sincerity of service and a lofty simplicity of life which is the austere flower of renunciation and self-sacrifice.

There are those who impatient and afraid of his exalted idealism would fain ignore him as fanatic, a mere fanciful dreamer of inconvenient and impossible dreams.

And yet, who can deny that this gentle and lowly apostle of passive resistance has more than a militant energy and courage and knows as Gokhale said how to "mould heroes out of common clay?"

Who can deny that this inexorable idealist who would reduce all life to an impersonal formula is the most vital personal force in the national movement and the prophet of Indian self-realization?

Foreword

He has mastered the secret of real greatness and learnt that true Yoga is wisdom in action and that love is the fulfilling of the law.

HYDERABAD,
DECCAN,
22nd Nov., 1917.

SAROJINI NAIDU

MOHANDAS KARAMCHAND GANDHI

A SKETCH OF HIS LIFE AND CAREER

THE figure of Mohandas Karamchand Gandhi is to-day a transfigured presence in the eyes of his countrymen. Like the unveiling of some sanctuary, where the high gods sit in session, or like some romance of the soul, is his career. The loftiest ideals of conduct of which man has dreamed are in him translated into actuality. He is the latest, though not the least, of the world's apostles. He seems for ever robed in vestments of shining white. Infinitely gentle, to the inner ear, is his footfall upon earth. His accents have the dewy freshness of the dawn. His brows are steeped in serenity and calm. His head is crowned with the martyr's crown. The radiance of the light spiritual encircles his whole being.

What shall it profit a man if he gain the whole world and lose his own scul! Return good for evil. Hatred ceases not by hatred but by love. How often has humanity in its long story listened to such exhortations! And yet how few are the sculs to whom they have ever carried the waters of life! To all men, surely, come glimpses of the highest. At the moment they touch our being with ecstasy and fade even before they are recognised. Not so with the great Ones of earth, the elect of God. They live their lives as ever before the altar. A divine inebriation is upon them and they can know no rest till they have drained the immortal cup to the dregs. The steeps they sight they needs must climb: and far down in the valley there kneels before them an adoring host of mortals.

The spontaneous and heartfelt reverence which Mr. Gandhi's name inspires to-day is a token that in him also India has recognised one such born priest of the ideal. The Sermon on the Mount may appear to many as gloriously impractical, but to Mr. Gandhi at least nothing is or ought to be more practical. To turn the left cheek when the right is beaten; to bless those that curse; to suffer for righteousness' sake; these are the very ideals to which he has surrendered his whole being. And by impassioned devotion to them he has developed a character before which men stand in awe. To the self-discipline of the ascetic he adds the sweetness and simplicity of a saint. The hero's will is in him wedded to the heart of a child. The service of man answers to the love of God. It was of such that it was said: *Ye are the salt of the earth.*

But how to write the life of such a man? How to tell the story of the soul's development? The task is impossible. The hopes and strivings of millions fulfil themselves in a single perfected character and to that extent the common man makes the hero and the apostle. The events of the personal drama simply register the rise and fall of consciousness; their explanation is outside them. In Mr. Gandhi's case, such a revelation came in the shape of the South African struggle. It was then that he burst upon the world as a moral force of the first order. That force itself had been long in preparing: how long who shall say? The story of that struggle with its shining roll of martyrs, both men and women, its thrilling incidents, marvellous pathos, and divine inspiration still waits for its destined chronicler. When he comes and throws it into terms of immortal literature it will assuredly take rank with the most memorable and resplendent chapters of its kind in history. It was an example and a demonstration of what one man can do by the sheer force of his character. It was likewise a demonstration of how masses of men and women, apparently lifeless and down-trodden, can develop astounding heroism under the impulsion of a truly great and selfless leader. The work done by Mr. Gandhi in South Africa must ever be reckoned amongst the greatest things accomplished by any single man. His life prior to his emergence on the South African stage was comparatively uneventful except for one or two glimpses of the coming greatness.

Mohandas Karamchand Gandhi was born on the 2nd of October 1869, the youngest of three children in a Vaishya family, at Porbander, a city of Kathiawar in Guzerat. Courage, administrative capacity, and piety were hereditary in the family. His immediate ancestors were in their way quite remarkable. His grand-father was Dewan of the Rana of Porbander, and an incident recorded of him shows what a fearless nature he had. Incurring the displeasure of the Queen who was acting as Regent for her son, he had actually to flee the Court of Porbander and take refuge with the Nawab of Junagadh who received him with great kindness. The courtiers of the Nawab observed and remarked that the ex-Dewan of Porbander gave his salute to the Nawab with his left hand in outrage of all convention. But the intrepid man replied, "Inspite of all that I have suffered I keep my right hand for Porbander still." Mr Gandhi's father was no less distinguished. Succeeding his father as Dewan of Porbander and losing like him the favour of the Ruling Chief, he repaired to Rajkot where he was entertained as Dewan. Here he rose rapidly in favour and such was the high regard which the Thakore Saheb of Rajkot came to have for him that he (theThakore Saheb) pressed his minister to accept a large grant of land in token of his esteem. But wealth had no attractions for him, and at first he declined the generous offer. Even when the entreaties of friends and relatives prevailed at last it was only a fraction of what was offered that he could be persuaded to accept. Even more interesting is another incident told of him. Happening to hear one day the Assistant Political Agent hold abusive language regarding the Thakore Sahib, he indignantly repudiated it. His Omnipotence the Political Agent demanded an apology which was stoutly refused. To rehabilitate his dignity the Assistant Political Agent thereupon ordered the offending Dewan to be arrested and detained under a tree for some hours! The apology was eventually waived and a reconciliation effected. Comment is needless. Mr. Gandhi's father was also a man of severe piety and could repeat the Baghavad Gita from end to end. His mother, however, was the most remarkable of all. Her influence on the character of her son has been profound and ineffaceable. Religion was the breath of her life. Long and rigorous were her fasts; many and lavish were her charities; and never could she brook to see a starving soul in her neighbourhood. Though in these respects she was typical of the Hindu woman, yet one feels that there must have been something unique about her. How else could she have been the mother of a Gandhi ?

In a home presided over by such a mother was his childhood passed. He was duly put to school at Porbander but a change occurring in its fortunes the whole family removed to Rajkot. Here the boy studied at first in a Vernacular school, and afterwards in the Kathiawar High School, whence he passed the matriculation examination at the age of seventeen. It may here be said that Mr. Gandhi was married as a boy of twelve to the noble soul who is now his partner in life and the glorified participator in all his sufferings and struggles.

An incident in his school life deserves more than ordinary mention. Born and bred in an atmosphere of uncompromising Vaishnavism, he had learned to perfection its ritual and worship, if not also to some extent, its rationale and doctrine. The principle of Ahimsa, non-killing (non-resistance to evil generally), is one of the keynotes of this teaching and Vaishnavas are, as a rule, strict vegetarians. But those were the days when even a schoolboy unconsciously imbibed a contempt for religion in general and for the ways of his forefathers in particular. Mr. Gandhi seems to have been no exception to this rule. Truth to say, the young Gandhi became a veritable sceptic even at the stage of his school career. This wreck of faith brought one disastrous consequence in its train. He and some school-companions of his came sincerely to believe that vegetarianism was a folly and superstition, and that to be civilised, the eating of flesh was essential. Nor were the boys slow to put their belief into action. Buying some flesh in secret every evening, they went to a secluded spot on the bank of a stream, cooked it and made a convivial meal. But Mr. Gandhi's conscience was all the while never at peace. At home he had to tell lies to excuse his lack of appetite and one subterfuge led to another. The boy loved truth and hated falsehood, and simply to avoid telling lies he abjured flesh-eating for ever. Truly the boy is father of the man!

After he passed the matriculation examination he was advised by a friend of the family to go to England and qualify himself for the Bar. His mother, however, would not listen to any such thing. Many a gruesome tale had the good woman heard of the abandoned nature of life in England and she shrank from the prospect of exposing her son to all its temptations as from the thought of hell. But the son was firm and the mother had to yield. But not until she had taken her son to a Jain Sannyasin and made him swear three solemn vows forswearing wine, flesh and women, did she give her consent.

Once in England Mr. Gandhi set about to make of himself a thorough 'English gentleman.' An Indian friend of his, then in England, who gloried in his anglicised ways took him in hand and gave lessons in fashion. Under his leadership he began to school himself in dancing, English music, and French, in fact in all the accomplishments needed for the great role of the 'English gentleman.' His heart, however, was never in the matter. The vows he had taken at his mother's instance haunted him strangely. One day he went to a party and there was served with flesh soup. It was a critical moment. His conscience swelled in protest and bade him make his choice on the spot between his three vows and the character of the English gentleman. And conscience won. Much to the chagrin of his friend before alluded to, he rose from the table and committed the great social sin of quitting the party abruptly. A great triumph for a youth! He thereafter bade adieu to all his newfangled ways: his feet ceased to dance, his fingers knew the violin no more, and the possibilities of the 'English gentleman' in him were lost for ever.

All this proved to be but the beginning of a keen spiritual struggle which stirred his being to its depths and out of which he emerged into an assured self-consciousness and abiding peace of soul. The eternal problems of existence now faced him and pressed for an answer. That this struggle was not merely intellectual, that it was no passing spasm such as even inferior men have known is proved by his subsequent career. As in the case of all great souls, his entire being was, we may take it, cast into the crucible to be melted and poured into divine moulds. The sense of an insufferable void within and without, that tribulation of the spirit which lays hands of torture upon the barred doors of the heart and unseals the inner vision—this it was that assailed him. At this critical time, friends were not wanting who tried to persuade him that in Christianity he would find the light for which he yearned. But these apparently did not meet with much success. At the same time he began to make a close study of the Bhagavad Gita, and it was the spiritual panorama which here was unveiled before him that finally stilled the commotion of his soul. It was here that he found the staff upon which he could lean. The void was now filled, light flooded his being and he had sensed the peace that passeth understanding. Hereafter the soul's endeavour was to be one, not of search, but realisation.

Mr. Gandhi's stay in England was otherwise uneventful. He passed the London Matriculation Examination, qualified himself for the Bar, and returned to India.

Melancholy news awaited his arrival in Bombay. Unknown to himself a calamity, which to a Hindu at least is one of the great calamities of life, had befallen him. His mother who had loved him as perhaps only a Hindu mother could, who had saved him from moral ruin, and who had doubtless winged ceaseless thoughts of love and prayer for her far-away son in England, that angel of a mother was no more. She had been dead sometime and the occurrence had been purposely kept a secret from him. We shall not attempt to describe his feelings when at last the news was disclosed to him.

The next eighteen months Mr. Gandhi spent,

partly at Bombay and partly at Rajkot, devoting himself to a deeper study of love and the Hindu scriptures. He also set up practice in the Bombay High Court. But there was other work to do for him in a different part of the world and the fates thus fulfilled themselves. A firm at Porbander which had a branch at Pretoria had an important law-suit in South Africa in which several Indians were concerned. The conduct of this suit expected to last for over a year being offered to him, he accepted it and proceeded to South Africa.

And here perhaps it will be fitting to envisage in general outline the position of the Indian immigrant in South Africa at the time. That position was frankly one of the utmost ignominy and injustice. More than half a century ago the colony of Natal wanted cheap labour for the development of its resources, and its eyes were turned to India as the best market for this supply. Representations were accordingly made to the Government of India through the Imperial Government and the indenture system was inaugurated. One gathers that in the early negotiations that went on between the Imperial and the Indian Governments on the question, solemn promises were made by the Imperial Government that the indentured immigrant would be treated with every consideration during the term of indenture and thereafter be accorded every facility to settle in South Africa if he so chose. But the way to a certain place is paved with good intentions and after a time the indenture system fast proved itself an abomination. Thousands of sturdy peasants from all parts of India, simple souls caught in the meshes of the recruiting agents by specious promises of a land flowing with milk and honey, found themselves on landing in South Africa waking up to a hopeless sense of anguish and disillusionment. The physical and moral conditions of life on the estates were ideally calculated to turn the very angels into brutes. The treatment accorded to the indentured labourer by his master was, to be as mild as possible, revolting in the extreme. The slave-owner was at least compelled by his selfishness to take care of the physical comfort of his human chattels but the employer of indentured labour was destitute of even this consideration! The tales of cruelty and individual suffering that has been collected and published almost tempt us to think that man was made not in the image of God but in that of His Ancient Enemy. And the most hopeless feature of the situation was that these victims of colonial greed were bound to serve their term and that they had no chance of laying, and much less of making good, any case against their masters. The laws themselves were unjust to the indentured labourer and were atrociously administered.

The position of the indentured labourer who had served his term and did not desire to re-enlist was one of calculated invidiousness. At every step he was hemmed in by a thousand obstacles thrown in his way and intended to frustrate any attempt to acquire a livelihood in freedom. Law and society conspired together to fix the brand of helotry to his brow. It was brought home to him in numberless ways that he was regarded as the member of some sub-human species, in whom it was sacrilege to defile the earth occupied by the white man, except as his hewer of wood and drawer of water. The law of the land here also did but reflect this dominant spirit of exclusiveness. It made distinctions between man and man on the ground of colour and race. In Natal, for instance, every ex-indentured Indian, man, woman, and child (boys and girls over a certain age) had to pay a poll tax of £3 per head. It is unnecessary, however to catalogue in detail the various disabilities legal, economic, political and social under which the Indian laboured.

The small body of professional people, lawyers, doctors, merchants, religious teachers, who followed in the wake of the indentured Indian, these also, whatever their position and culture, fell equally under the same ban. The coloured man was in the eyes of the white colonist in South Africa a vile and accursed thing. There could be no distinction here of high and low. If these colonials had been asked to paint God they would have painted him white! There were certain differences in the position of the Indian between one province and another, in South Africa itself, the ideal in this line having been attained in the Transvaal and the Orange Free State, then independent. Not to labour the tale throughout South Africa the law was unjust to the Indian and man inhuman.

It is however interesting to think what a medley of elements contributed to this attitude. First and foremost, there was the antipathy of colour and race—to what lengths this can go in the modern civilized West, the American institution of lynching sufficiently illustrates. Secondly, there was the economic factor—the free Indian was a formidable competitor in trade to the small white dealer. His habits were simple, his life temperate, and he was able to sell things much more cheaply. Thirdly, there was the instinct of earth-monopoly—South Africa must be and continue to remain a white man's land. Lastly, there was a vague feeling that the influx of the coloured man was a growing menace to the civilization of the white. The solution of the problem from the point of view of the South African colonist was very simple—to prohibit all immigration in the future, and to make the position of those that already had come so intolerable as to drive them to repatriate themselves. And towards this end, forces were inwardly making in South Africa when Mr. Gandhi first landed there. The paradox of the whole thing lay in the fact, that while India had been asking for the Indian, in South Africa, the elementary rights of a British citizen, the colonial was all the while thinking of casting him out for ever as an unclean thing.

From the very day that Mr. Gandhi set foot

Mr. GANDHI Barrister.

XXI

at Natal he had to taste of the bitter cup of humiliation which was then the Indian's portion. At court he was rudely ordered to remove the barrister's turban he had on, and he left the court at once burning with mortification. This experience, however, was soon eclipsed by a host of others still more ignominous. Journeying to the Transvaal in a railway train, the guard unceremoniously ordered him to quit the first-class compartment, though he had paid for it, and betake himself to the van. Refusing, he was brutally dragged out with his luggage. And the train at once steamed off. All this was on British soil! In the Transvaal itself things were even worse. As he was sitting on the box of a coach on the way to Pretoria, the guard asked him to dismount because he wanted to smoke there. A refusal brought two consecutive blows in quick succession. In Pretoria he was once kicked off a foot-path by a sentry. The catalogue may be still further extended, but it would be a weariness of the flesh.

The law suit which he had been engaged to conduct was at last over, and a social gathering was given in his honour on the eve of his departure for India. That evening

Mr. Gandhi chanced to see a local newspaper which announced that a bill was about to be introduced into the colonial Parliament to disfranchise Indians and that other bills of a similar character were soon to follow. With true insight he immediately perceived the gravity of the situation, and explained to the assembled guests that if the Indian community in South Africa was to be saved from utter extinction immediate and resolute action should be taken. At his instance a message was at once sent to the colonial Parliament requesting delay of proceedings, which was soon followed up by a largely signed petition against the new measure. But all this was of no avail. The bill was passed in due course. Now another largely signed petition was sent to the Colonial Secretary in England, and in consequence the Royal Assent was withheld. But this again was of no avail for the same goal was reached by a new bill through a slightly different route. Now it was that Mr. Gandhi seriously mooted the question of a central organization in South Africa to keep vigilant watch over Indian interests. But it was represented to him that such an organization would be impossible unless he himself consented to remain in South Africa. The prominent Indians guaranteed him a practice if he should choose to stay. In response to their wishes he enrolled himself in the Supreme Court of Natal though not without some objection, at first, on the ground of his colour. Thus began for him that long association with South Africa which was destined to have such memorable results.

From a moral point of view the choice that he made to remain in South Africa, to which he had gone only on a temporary professional visit, was the first great act of Mr. Gandhi's public career. A young man with his life before him and every prospect of carving distinction for himself in his own native land is called upon to brush all that aside and devote himself to the uplift of his own countrymen in a far away land amidst circumstances of disgusting humiliation and struggle. How many in Mr. Gandhi's position would have made the same choice ? How many would have had the same passivity to surrender themselves to the guiding hand of destiny ? How many would have placed service above self? But to men born for great ends such crises of the soul come only to find them prepared. The South African Indian community were like a flock of sheep without a shepherd, surrounded by ravenous wolves, and Mr. Gandhi chose to be the shepherd. South Africa was the vine-yard of the Lord in which he was called upon to dig and delve, and he chose to be the labourer. From the day that his resolve was taken he consecrated himself to his work as to a high and lofty mission.

His first step, was to make his countrymen in South Africa articulate. And with this object he organised them into various societies all over the land. He trained them in methods of constitutional agitation and for the purpose held meetings and conferences, and promoted petitions and memorials. He also sought out young men willing and capable and trained them for public work. And it was his character that imparted vitality to all his endeavours. By mixing with high and low on equal terms, by his readiness to succour the needy and console the afflicted, by the example he set of a simple, pure and austere life, by his transparent sincerity and perfect selflessness he made a profound impression upon them all and acquired an influence which deepened in the passage of the years into a boundless reverence. Nor should it be forgotten that, that amongst the European community itself there were some good men and true who saw and recognised in him a soul of transcendent goodness.

In the year 1896 Mr. Gandhi came to India to take his wife and children to South Africa. Before he left South Africa he wrote and published an 'open letter' detailing the wrongs and grievances of his countrymen resident there.

News of the splendid work which he had done in South Africa had travelled before him to India, and Indians of all classes joined in according him an enthusiastic reception wherever he went. In these meetings Mr. Gandhi had of course to make some speeches. Our good friend, Reuter, sent highly garbled versions of his addresses to South Africa. He was represented as telling his Indian audiences that Indians in South Africa were uniformly treated like wild beasts. The blood of the Colonials was up and the feeling against Mr. Gandhi reached white heat. Meeting after meeting was held in which he was denounced in the most scathing terms. Meanwhile he was urgently requested to return to Natal without a moment's delay, and he embarked accordingly.

The steamer carrying Mr. Gandhi reached Durban on the same day as another steamer, which had left Bombay with 600 Indian passengers on board two days after Mr. Gandhi's own departure. The two ships were immediately quarantined indefinitely. Great things were transpiring at Durban meanwhile. The Colonials were determined not to land the Asiatics. Gigantic demonstrations were taking place, and the expediency of sending the Indians back was gravely discussed. It was plain that the Colonials would go any length to accomplish their purpose. The more boisterous spirits even proposed the sinking of the ship. Word was sent to Mr. Gandhi that if he and his compatriots should attempt to land they should do so at infinite peril; but threats were of no avail. On the day on which the new Indian arrivals were expected to land a huge concourse had assembled at the docks. There was no end of hissing, shouting, roaring and cursing. The Attorney-General of Natal addressed the infuriate gathering and promised them that the matter would receive the early attention of Parliament, commanding them at the same time in the name of the Queen to disperse. And the crowd dispersed. Mr. Gandhi came ashore sometime after the landing of his fellow-passengers, having previously sent his wife and children to the house of a friend. He was immediately recognised by some of the stragglers who at once began to set up a howl. A rickshaw was engaged, but the way was blocked. Mr. Gandhi walked on foot with a European friend and when they reached one of the streets the pressure was so great that the two friends were separated. The crowd at once began to maul Mr. Gandhi till the Police came and took him to the house of a friend. The Police Superintendent expressed his apprehensions that the mob in their frenzy would even set fire to the house. Mr. Gandhi was obliged to dress himself as a Police constable and take refuge in the Police Station. This ebullition of abnormal feeling subsided after some time and a momentous page in Mr. Gandhi's life was turned.

In October 1899 war broke out between the English and the Boers in South Africa. Mr. Gandhi, with the sagacity of a true leader at once perceived what a golden opportunity it was to the British Indians to vindicate their self-respect and readiness to suffer in the cause of the Empire. At his call hundreds of his countrymen in South Africa were glad to enlist themselves as Volunteers, but the offer was rejected with scorn by the powers that be. The offer was renewed a second time, only to meet with a similar fate. When however the British arms sustained some disasters, it was recognised that every man available should be put into the field and Mr. Gandhi's offer on behalf of his compatriots was accepted. A thousand Indians came forward, and were constituted into an Ambulance Corps, to assist in carrying the wounded to the hospitals. Of the service that was rendered in that direction, it is not necessary to speak as it has been recognised even in South Africa. At another time the British Indians were employed to receive the wounded out of the line of fire and carry them to a place more than twenty miles off. When the battle was raging, Major Bapte who was commanding came to Mr. Gandhi who of course was one of the Volunteers, and represented that if they worked from within the line of the fire they should be rendering inestimable service. At once all the Indian Volunteers responded to the request and dauntlessly exposed themselves to shot and shell. Many an Indian life was lost that day.

The war was over and the Transvaal became a part of the British Empire. Mr. Gandhi was under the impression that, since the wrongs of the British Indian subjects of the Queen were one of the declared causes of the war, under the new Government those wrongs would be a thing of the past. And accordingly he returned to India with no idea of going back, but he was reckoning without his host. The little finger of the new Government was thicker than the loins of the Boers. The Boers had indeed stung the Indian subjects of the Queen with whips but the new Government stung them with scorpions. A new Asiatic department was constituted to deal with Asiatics as a species apart. A most insidious policy of exclusion was maturing. The prospect was dark and appalling and Mr. Gandhi had to return to the scene of his labours. He interviewed the authorities but he was assured that he had no business to interfere in the matter while they themselves were there to look after everything. Mr. Joseph Chamberlain was then in South Africa and a deputation led by Mr. Gandhi waited upon him in Natal. In Pretoria however a similar deputation was disallowed unless Mr. Gandhi was excluded. Evidently Mr. Gandhi's name was becoming gall and worm-wood to the authorities. But he was not the man to be frightened. He determined to fight out the battle in the Law Courts and enrolled himself on the Supreme Court of Pretoria.

He now felt more than ever the imperative need of an organ which should at once educate the South African Indian community on the one hand and be on the other the faithful mouth-piece of their views. In 1903 a press was bought and the paper "Indian Opinion" was ushered into existence. It was published in four languages, English, Tamil, Guzerati and Hindi. At first it didn't prove a success and entailed such heavy loss that during the first year alone Mr. Gandhi had to pay a sum of £ 2,000 out of his own pocket. Though in subsequent years the financial position of the paper has somewhat improved, it has never been a pecuniary success. Notwithstanding, it has grown to be a great force in South Africa and rendered invaluable service during the recent struggle.

In the year 1904 a virulent attack of plague broke out among the Indian Community in Johannesburg. The Municipal authorities were either ignorant or apathetic. Mr. Gandhi, however, was at once on the scene and sent word to the authorities that if immediate action were not taken an epidemic was in prospect. But no answer came. One day the plague carried off as many as twenty-one victims. Mr. Gandhi with three or four noble comrades at once broke open one of the Indian stores which was empty, and had the patients carried there and did what he could in the matter. The next morning the Municipal authorities bestirred themselves and took the necessary action. The plague lasted a month counting more than a hundred victims. We in India may shudder to think to what an appalling magnitude the outbreak may have grown but for the heroic endeavours of the subject of this sketch, and his devoted comrades. In such ways, indeed, had Mr. Gandhi's influence begun to bear fruit.

It was about this time also that Mr. Gandhi founded the famous "Phoenix Settlement." He had been reading Ruskin's *Unto this Last* and its influence sank deep into his mind.

He was at once on fire with the author's idea of country settlements and shortly after the plague subsided, Mr. Gandhi went to Natal and purchased a piece of land at Phœnix, a place situated "on the hill sides of a rich grassy country." Houses were built and a village sprang up on the mountain side. In this 'settlement' Mr. Gandhi sought to enshrine his ideal of the simple life. It was to be a retreat from the bustle of city life where men and women might by communion with nature seek to divest their life and mind of all artificial trappings and come nearer to the source of their own being. It was to be an ashrama, a spot of sanctity and peace. Its members were to be a spiritual brotherhood and were to know no differences of rank. To all alike labour was to be a privilege and a joy. All had to dig, plough and cultivate the adjoining land with their own hands. Mr. Gandhi himself when he was in South Africa used to go to the village during his moments of leisure and take part in the work of cultivation like anybody else. But he had to fulfil this sublime idealistic impulse of his at immense pecuniary sacrifice, for the scheme, we are told "absolutely impoverished him."

It was here also that Mr. Gandhi practised a great *tapasya.* Here he laid upon himself and his family the yoke of an iron discipline in daily habit. He stripped himself of all luxury in externals. He wore the coarsest raiment and for food took only so much as would suffice to keep body and soul together. He slept upon a coarse blanket in the open air. He starved the flesh and reined in the mind. And his soul waxed in joy and strength. And to those that beheld it was a marvel and a wonder.

In 1906 the Zulus broke out in rebellion and a corps of twenty Indians with Mr. Gandhi as leader was formed to help to carry the wounded to the hospital. The corps subsequently acted as nurses and Mr. Gandhi ministered in person to the wounded Zulus. The founding of the Phœnix Ashrama and the nursing of the Zulus with all their meaning in terms of the higher life were a fitting prelude to what was about to follow.

In the year 1906 the new Government of the Transvaal brought forward a new law affecting all Asiatics, which was sinister, retrograde and obnoxious in the last degree. One morning all the children of Asia in the Transvaal awoke and found themselves called upon to register themselves anew by giving thumb impressions. Thus all Asiatics were placed on a level with convicts. And yet these light-hearted legislators and their compatriots were by profession the flock of an Asiatic whose injunction to his disciples was to go forth amongst the children of men as lambs amongst wolves! Who will dare to say that in the dealings of the western nations with 'coloured' races this spirit has ever been much in evidence? How else could these colonials have so merrily blackened a whole continent which has been the home of the oldest civilisations and has given to humanity its greatest prophets and saviours? But in this case also the Asiatic lambs were destined to give a glorious object-lesson to the wolves.

The object of the new measure was apparently to prevent unlawful immigration from what they regarded as the pariah continent. Now the Indian Community throughout South Africa and their leaders were quite willing that reasonable restrictions should be placed on all future immigration though on abstract considerations of justice they could have insisted upon the right of the 'open door.' But what they had been agitating against all these years and what they could not reconcile themselves to was that this object should be compassed by laws which tended to differentiate them on any ground of colour or race. The principle of equality of all races before the law, however much its application may have to be tempered by considerations of circumstance, had been the very head and front of their demands. And now defiance and contempt were hurled at them in the shape of this new law. It was at the same time a certainty that it was but the precursor in the Transvaal and in other parts of South Africa of more insidious and flagrant measures intended to drive out the Indian Community once and for ever. And it was hailed by the colonials as the beginning of the end, while the Indian Community was convulsed with indignation.

Meanwhile Mr. Gandhi and his co-workers were not idle. They proceeded to interview the member of the Government in charge of the new bill, but when they succeeded only in getting women excluded from its operation it was realised that there was now nothing left for persuasion to accomplish. The

Legislative Council passed the new measure after the farce of a discussion. Infinitely more important to us are the proceedings of another meeting held in that very city and at the very time when the bill was being rushed through the council. It is an immense gathering, consisting of several thousands of Indians of all classes and creeds. A great spirit animates all. Impassioned speeches are made denouncing the new law. But now at the close the great throng rises up and shouts a solemn 'Amen.' It is the vow of passive resistance that he has thus been administered. Those thousands had decided not against the new bill but against the new Act. They had decided also that henceforth they were to be the masters of their own fate and not General Smuts or Botha or the Legislative Council. And the onlooker may well have whispered to himself, "To-day we have been present at the lighting of a fire which will never go out."

It was a momentous step. But Mr. Gandhi on whom the burden of leadership now lay heavily was eager to take any step that promised an alternative solution. And accordingly a deputation under his leadership and that of Mr. Ali was sent to England to agitate, if possible, against the Royal Assent being given to the new legislation. The Royal Assent was withheld in consequence till a constitutional Government should be installed in the Transvaal. As a result of its efforts a committee in London with Lord Amphthill, ex-Governor of Madras, as President, Sir Mancherjee Bowanaggree as Executive Chairman, and Mr. Ritch as Secretary, was also formed to keep guard over Indian interests in South Africa. But the relief thus obtained was only temporary. A constitutional Government was soon formed in the Transvaal, the new measure was passed in hot haste, received the Royal Assent, and became law.

Thus was the Indian community in the Transvaal impelled upon the great destiny of 'passive resistance.' To register or not to register was now the question: to register and sell their honour and self-respect for a mess of pottage or not to register and take up arms against a 'sea of troubles.' Like the voice of God speaking to the inmost soul was Mr. Gandhi's appeal to his countrymen at this hour. There could be no question, he explained, of their submitting to this final and crowning challenge of colonial insolence to Indian manhood. There was nothing left but to bare the majesty of their own souls to the storm and defy it to do its utmost. The prison and the gaol were now to be the cells of their own self-discipline. All the forces of darkness in league were powerless to move them from the firm-set purpose of their own hearts. Was spirit greater than matter? Was the body to be nailed to the cross or the soul? Was not Heaven itself beckoning them to the great Heights? In such wise did Mr. Gandhi adjure his countrymen.

The words of the leader awoke a responsive thrill in thousands of intrepid hearts. Like one man they vowed against the registration. Like one man they resolved to face prosecution and persecution, dungeon and death itself. Like one man they resolved to make atonement for the heaped-up humiliations of many years by a supreme and triumphant act of self-vindication which should rivet the eyes of the whole world. The hour of the spirit's rebound when individuals and communities alike cleave through every consideration save that of their own integrity, that hour had come.

The passive resistance movement had commenced. The registering officers went about from place to place, but little business had they to do as ninety-five per cent. of the people remained true to their oath. The law took its course and a veritable saturnalia of imprisonments ensued. The gaols became literally crammed with the Indians who suffered for conscience' sake. High and low, rich and poor went to the gaol as to the bridal. Husband was separated from wife, child from parent, and yet the fervour and pertinacity of the sufferers abated not. Mr. Gandhi himself was sentenced to two months' simple imprisonment. During the trial he took full responsibility for the course adopted by the Indian community and asked for the maximum punishment for himself. The authorities were naturally perturbed to see the worm turning and for the first time displayed a chastened mood. Negotiations were opened through the mediation of one, Mr. Cartwright, a journalist, and it was agreed that the new law should be suspended for three months, that in the meanwhile registration should be made voluntarily, and that at the end of the period it should be repealed. In pursuance of this arrangement Mr. Gandhi himself, to set an example, went to the office to register. The position of a leader is fraught with peril, and a Pathan who had joined the passive resistance movement imagined that Mr. Gandhi was playing the coward and betraying his trust. Under this impression he dealt him such severe blows on his way to the registration office that he instantly fell down senseless on the spot. As a result of the injuries received he hovered between life and death for some time, during which the wife of his good friend and admirer, the Rev. Mr. Doke, a baptist minister of Johannesburg, devotedly nursed him back to life. His friends afterwards asked him to take legal action against the Pathan but he replied that the Pathan had done only what he considered to be right! This incident threw the situation into confusion for the moment but subsequently the process of voluntary registration was satisfactorily completed and the authorities were called upon to perform their part of the compact. But this they refused to do, and all efforts at compromise proving futile there was now no alternative but to resume the struggle.

MRS. J. J. DOKE,
Who Nursed Mr. Gandhi after the assault
by a Pathan in 1908.

MRS. H. S. L. POLAK,
The Founder of the Transvaal Indian
Women's Association.

Once more did the rapture of suffering come upon thousands and the prison-house become a holy of holies. And how glorious was the spirit which had come upon them! Gentle and meek and uncomplaining, it was the very spirit of that Cross which their persecutors professed to follow but honoured so little in practice. It was almost as if one heard these men exclaim, "Lord, forgive them, for they know not what they do." From every class and sect were the heroes drawn. Many among them were the poorest of the poor, living by the sweat of the brow and innocent of 'education.' Wealthy merchants went into voluntary insolvency rather than prove false to their vow. The ruin and misery caused, the dislocation of family life, the hunger and starvation of the women and children were indescribable. But the women amidst all the desolation of their hearts only cheered the men on! The passive resisters were subjected to cruel hardships and indignities in gaol that their spirit might be broken, but this served only to quicken and intensify it. They had tasted of an immortal cup and anguish itself had now become only the food of their souls.

To us in Southern India it is a matter

for splendid pride that amongst them all none displayed greater resolution or a more indomitable fibre than the children of the Tamil land. It has been calculated that out of a total population of nine thousand male Indians in the Transvaal two thousand seven hundred had in this way suffered 'untold miseries in prison,' and many of them again and again. Needless to say, Mr. Gandhi himself was one of the victims this time also, being sentenced to a term of two months with hard labour. We have no space to refer to the hardships he endured with his brother sufferers in jail, to his many acts of self-denial, and to the sublime manner in which he bore up, believing as he did that suffering is the heaven-ordained path to perfection. That so many should have been consumed by the apostolic fire and should have so clearly realised the issues at stake is a tribute at once to the relentless fury of the persecutors, the spiritual force of Mr. Gandhi, and the greatness of common human nature.

After his release from his second term of imprisonment Mr. Gandhi organised two deputations, one to England and the other to India for the purpose of educating public opinion in both countries. Several of the delegates were arrested on the eve of their departure and sentenced to prison as passive resisters. But Mr. Gandhi and some others nevertheless went to England and were successful in awakening some interest in the matter. The Transvaal ministers were then in England and the Imperial authorities tried to bring about a settlement. But General Smuts was implacable and nothing worth mentioning came of it. Arrangements were however made for a body of volunteers who undertook to collect funds and keep public interest alive, and the deputation returned to South Africa.

The deputation to India consisted of but one individual, that doughty and indefatigable champion of the Indian cause in South Africa, and Editor of the paper '*Indian Opinion*,' Mr. H. S. L. Polak. Feeling in India had reached a high pitch of resentment against the policy of the Transvaal Government even before his arrival. But when he under the direction of the late Mr. Gokhale toured the country and narrated in dozens of meetings the heart-rending tale of the South African persecution that feeling easily reached boiling-point and the demand for reprisals came from every quarter of the land. Funds also came pouring in for the relief of the distressed children in a far-away land who had done so much to raise their motherland in the estimation of the world.

One great and immediate result of Mr. Polak's propaganda was that attention in India was concentrated upon the enormities of the Indenture system as never it had been concentrated before. And when in March 1912 the late Mr. Gokhale moved in the Imperial Legislative Council a resolution for its abolition in a speech of classic force and dignity, the Government of India had to bow to Indian public opinion and signify acceptance. It was the first great victory of the Passive Resistance movement.

In South Africa itself the movement had a two-fold reaction. On the one hand, it made an indelible impression upon the better mind of the colonial and this found expression in the formation of a committee called the Hosken Committee, under the presidency of Sir William Hosken, a good, ardent and noble man, who in the face of obloquy from his own countrymen expoused the Indian cause with a zeal that was above all praise. On the other hand, it spurred the authorities to that increasing vindictiveness which imagines that the soul could be coerced by a more thoroughgoing application of brute force.

With the blindness that has characterised the persecutor in history the authorities in the Transvaal strengthened their hands by a new power, *viz.*, that of deportation, hoping thereby to foil the Passive Resister. At first they deported the more prominent of them across the Natal border but these returned as fast as they were sent out. Not to be baulked the authorities now went the length of deporting a good many of the passive resisters, about sixty-four in number, all the way to India. But these again were sent back with the sympathy and admiration of a whole nation. Utterly lost to all sense of shame the Transvaal authorities by hook and by crook did their level best to prevent them from landing. And one of the returning deportees, a lion-hearted youth Narayanaswamy, by name, hunted in this way from one British port to another died in Delgoa Bay in Portuguese territory. And his martyr-death threw a fresh halo of sanctity over the cause. The Government of India greatly impressed by the gravity of the situation in India consequent on the Transvaal occurrences moved the Imperial Government in England, who in their turn did their best to woo the Transvaalies to a more conciliatory mood. And the result was that the deportation process subsequently stopped.

After the various provinces of South Africa had been constituted into the South African Union the Imperial Government in England at the insistence of the Government of India strove once more to persuade the Union Government to effect a reasonable settlement of the problem, and for the purpose, addressed to the latter a despatch in October 1910, recommending the repeal of the law which had been the origin of the whole trouble, and the adoption of legislation on non-racial lines which, while prohibiting all future immigration in effect, will yet leave room for the entry into South Africa of a small and defined minimum of educated people. At the same time the Imperial Government pointed out that any such law should not have the effect of taking away any rights till then enjoyed by immigrants in the coast-lying provinces. This time the Union Government were willing to consider the suggestion, and to give effect thereto brought forward the Union Immigration Bill in 1911, which while repealing the old law did not annul the racial distinction, and further took away several rights from the residents of the coast districts—the very thing deprecated by the Imperial Government. This bill was naturally unacceptable to the Indian Community and finally was not passed. An understanding however was arrived at by which the passive resisters agreed to suspend their movement, and the authorities agreed to introduce satisfactory legislation in 1912, meanwhile administering the law as though it had been already altered. The measure of 1912 was however no better and the truce was extended for one more year. It was then that Mr. Gandhi invited the late Mr. Gokhale to South Africa to study the whole situation on the spot, and the latter with the full approval of the Indian and Imperial Governments sailed for that country and arrived at Capetown on 22nd October, 1912. He stayed for about three weeks and toured the whole country visiting every important city. Everywhere he was received with signal honour, not merely by the Indian community but also by the colonial authorities themselves, and succeeded in making a great impression by that sweet reasonableness for which he was so well-known. He interviewed the Union ministers and secured from them the promise of a satisfactory settlement, and amongst other things the repeal of the £3 tax which every ex-indentured Indian man and woman had to pay in Natal, and to which reference has been made already. Things seemed to augur well for the future and hope began to revive where despair had reigned before.

A fresh and extraordinary complication was now introduced into the situation in the shape of a judicial decision of the Union Court which declared all Indian marriages to be null and void under the law of the Union. The consternation into which it plunged the entire Indian Community is imagined than described. When the long-expected legislation was at last introduced into the Union Parliament in 1913, it was evident that it was merely tinkering with the whole problem without any attempt at solving it in a liberal or large-hearted manner. Warnings were accordingly given and representations made

MR. H. KALLENBACH,
The owner of Tolstoy Farm. Great Helper of Indians in their distress, joint organiser of the Strikers' Camp and a Passive Resister.

MR. H. S. L. POLAK,
Editor Indian Opinion. A Passive Resister who went as delegate to India and England.

to the authorities by the Indian leaders but to no purpose. A few amendments were made in the original bill but the Act as passed was absolutely inadequate to meet the requirements of the situation. At this juncture a deputation was sent to England to bring home to the Imperial authorities and the British public the profound danger of the whole position, and the certainty that if timely steps were not taken it would lead to the revival of passive resistance on a vastly enlarged scale. But it was in vain. It required still an appalling amount of suffering before the conscience of the Union could at all be moved.

The struggle accordingly recommenced with a grimness and determination which threw into the shade even the previous campaigns. The principal planks of the passive resister this time were, the abolition of the £3 tax, the complete eradication of the racial bar as a principle of legislation, the recognition of the validity of Indian marriages, the right of entry into Cape Colony of all South Africa-born Indians, and the sympathetic and equitable administration of all laws affecting the British Indian immigrant.

Of the incidents of this final stage of the struggle one can speak only in terms of bated breath. For it had been decreed that the baptism of fire through which the Indian Community had been passing during these long years should now be bestowed on the only two classes which had hitherto remained outside it—the women and the indentured labourer. The Indian women in the Transvaal had indeed already played a memorable part, by the fine understanding they had displayed of the purposes of the whole movement, and by the whole-hearted sympathy and encouragement which they had given to their men-folk. But the time had now come for the women themselves to step into the flaming breach. Like an arrow in the heart did they receive the judicial dictum which pronounced their marriages to be invalid. Or rather it was that the entrance of this arrow was but the occasion for the opening of the flood-gates of that idealism of which woman's heart is the chosen home. And in what a deluge did it thereafter pour! How many hundreds were the Indian women that sanctified the prison-houses of South Africa! And how superb was the intoxication that came upon the men-folk as they beheld their own mothers, wives and sisters mock at the crucifixion of the body! Never before in the history of the world had a more signal proof been given of the power of the human soul to defy the arrayed forces of wickedness and embrace suffering in the battle for honour and self-respect. The splendour and ecstasy of it all will last through the ages.

The account given by Mrs. Polak in the pages of 'Indian Opinion' of the part played by women in the struggle is so interesting that it deserves to be quoted in full. She writes :—

"Ruskin has said: "A woman's duty is two-fold, her duty to her home and her duty to the State." Scarcely an Indian woman in South Africa has read Ruskin's words, probably never heard of them, but the spirit of truth manifests itself in many ways and places, and the Indian women of South Africa intuitively knew this as one of the true laws of life, and their work showed that they performed their greater duty accordingly. These women, without any training for public life, accustomed to the retirement of women of India, not versed or read in the science of sociology, just patient, dutiful wives, mothers, and daughters of a struggling class of workers, in an hour of need, moved by the spirit of a larger life, took up their duty to their country, and served it with that heroism of which such women alone are capable.

It is said so often that woman does not reason, and perhaps it is a charge largely true, but where the elementary laws of being are concerned, woman follows a surer path than any dictated by reason, and sooner or later gets to her goal. Every reform movement has shown that, from the moment women stand side by side with men in the maintenance of a principle, however dimly understood by them, the spirit of the movement grows, is crystallised, and success to the movement is assured.

The Western is so accustomed to think of the Indian woman as one living in retirement, without any broad thought and without any interest in public affairs, that it must have come with a shock of surprise to learn that many Indian women, some with babies in their arms, some expecting babies to be born to them, and some quite young girls, were leaving their homes and taking part in all the hardships of the Passive Resistance campaign.

The last phase of the fight, and the one through which to-day we rejoice in peace, was practically led in the early stages by a small band of women from Natal, who challenged prison to vindicate their right to the legal recognition of their wifehood, and a similar small band of women from Johannesburg.

The women from Natal, all of them wives of wellknown members of the Indian community, travelled up to Volksrust, were arrested and sentenced to three months' hard labour, and were the first of hundreds to go to gaol. The women from the Transvaal travelled down the line, taking in the mines on their way, holding meetings and calling upon the men to refuse to work and to die rather than live as slaves, and at the call of these women, thousands laid down their tools and went on strike. I think it may safely be said that, but for the early work of these brave women, during the middle of last year, the wonderful response to the call of honour and country might never have taken place. About six weeks after the Transvaal women left, they also were arrested, and a similar sentence to that passed upon the women of Natal was passed upon them, and they were forcibly vaccinated. So these brave women were shut away from life, but the fight now so splendidly begun went on.

A few days after the release of these last women, two gave birth to children, and another, a young girl of about twenty, passed away, and a third hovered between life and death for months, but the goal was won. To-day, all these women are back in their homes and are busy in the usual routine of an Indian woman's life. There is absolutely none of the pride of heroism about them. They are the same patient, dutiful women that India has produced for centuries; yet they endured the publicity, and no one who does not know India can understand how terrible to the Indian woman such publicity is. They endured the physical hardship, the mental sorrow, the heartache; for nearly all who did not take young children with them left young ones at home, endured hunger strikes, because they were deprived of fat to eat and sandals to put on—endured it all without harshness or bitterness. India has many things to be proud of, but of none more than the part the Indian women of South Africa took in the uplifting and recognition of a people here despised."

The foregoing account refers to a strike on the coal-mines. The organization of a strike of the Indentured labourers was part and parcel of the scheme of the leaders for the final campaign. This strike and the famous march of the strikers to the Transvaal, we cannot better describe than in the words of an article entitled "That Wonderful March" in that self-same journal. It runs :—

"The question of the repeal of the £3 tax had become urgent already in 1908 and 1909, when an organisation had been formed for the purpose of securing it, and petitions widely signed had been sent to the then Natal Parliament, without other result than the passing of the ineffective Act of 1910, giving magistrates discretion—which some used, while others did not—to exempt certain classes of women in certain circumstances.

During his campaign in India, in 1909-10 and 1911-12, and his visit to England in 1911, Mr. Polak had pressed the question upon the attention of the people and Government of India and the British public, who had hitherto been ignorant as to the harsh incidence of the tax and grim misery that it entailed.

Accordingly, when the Hon. Mr. Gokhale came to South Africa in 1912, and set himself to the task of examining Indian grievances on the spot, he immediately seized upon the tax as one that required and was capable of immediate remedy, and he, therefore, as he has told us, made special representations on the subject at the meeting of Ministers at Pretoria, when, he is positive, a definite undertaking was given him to repeal the tax. His efforts to that end had already been foreshadowed whilst he had travelled through the Union, and he had given assurances to vast crowds of those liable to the tax that he would not rest until he had secured its repeal, a resolve that had been much encouraged by the sympathetic speeches and conversations of prominent Natalians, both at the Durban banquet and at the subsequent Chamber of Commerce meeting. And these promises, fortified by the knowledge of what had transpired at Pretoria, Mr. Gandhi, upon his return from Zanzibar, whither he had accompanied Mr. Gokhale, repeated again and again in a responsible manner, to large numbers of those affected by the tax.

When, therefore, in 1913, a measure was introduced into the Union Parliament, at the end of the session, exempting women only from its operation, but requiring them to take out an annual licence, a message was sent to Mr. Gokhale in India requiring whether the promise of repeal had been limited to women. The reply was that it applied to all who were affected by the tax, and the Bill was promptly killed by Mr. Meyler and the late Sir David Hunter, who protested against its further progress, as they felt convinced that to pass it would be to delay total repeal indefinitely. Up to this time there had been no denial by the Government of the promise alleged.

At the rising of Parliament, Mr. Gandhi entered into fresh negotiations with the Union Government, reminding them of the promise, and asking for a definite undertaking of repeal of the tax in 1914. Meanwhile, in England, Mr. Polak, who had gone there at Mr. Gokhale's instance, had made it clear to the Imperial authorities and the British public that, whilst the repeal of the £3 tax had not previously formed part of the Passive Resisters' demands, the question had now become so acute, and Indian public feeling in South Africa had become so intense owing to what was regarded as the Union Government's breach of faith that, in the unfortunate event of the revival of the struggle, repeal of the tax would be made part and parcel of it. Lord Ampthill, too, after consulting with Mr. Gokhale, referred in explicit terms to the promise of repeal, in a portentous speech in the House of Lords. In the result, the Union Government declined to give an undertaking on the subject, though they still did not deny the promise, and the question therefore. formed one of the five points of Passive Resistance in Mr. A. M. Cachalia's letter of the 12th September, announcing the revival of the struggle. At the same time, Mr. Gokhale, in the face of the objections of his medical advisers, hurried back to India to rouse the Government and his fellow-countrymen to action.

On September 28, and before any important activity had developed Mr. Gandhi addressed to the Secretary for the Interior a letter containing the following warning and appeal :—

"I know also what responsibility lies on my shoulders in advising such a momentous step, but I feel that it is not possible for me to refrain from advising a step which I consider to be necessary, to be of educational value, and, in the end, to be valuable both to the Indian community and to the State. This step consists in actively, persistently, and continuously asking those who are liable to pay the £3 tax to decline to do so and to suffer the penalties for non-payment, and what is more important; in asking those who are now serving indenture and who will, therefore, be liable to pay the £3 Tax upon the completion of their indenture, to strike work until the tax is withdrawn. I feel that in view of Lord Ampthill's declaration in the House of Lords, evidently with the approval of Mr. Gokhale, as to the definite promise made by the Government and repeated to Lord Gladstone, this advice to indentured Indians would be fully justified. . . . Can I not even now, whilst in the midst of the struggle, appeal to General Smuts and ask him to reconsider his decision . . . . on the question of the £3 tax?" The letter was shown to General Smuts who vouchsafed no reply, but who also did not even then repudiate the promise, nor did he warn the employers of the intentions of the Passive

Resistance leaders. A fortnight later, in a statement circulated by Reuter's Agency throughout the South African press, it was clearly stated that "the movement will also consist in advising indentured Indians to suspend work until the £3 Tax is removed. The indentured Indians will not be invited to join the general struggle." The public thus received ample warning of what was toward.

The Indian women who had joined the struggle as a protest against the refusal of the Government to legalise Indian marriages and who, as Passive Resisters, had unsuccessfully sought imprisonment at Vereeniging, Germiston and Volksrust, were allowed to pass into Natal unmolested, and the first steps taken to "call out" the Indians on the coal-mines in the northern part of the Province were due to the courage and devotion of these women, whose appearance there was almost in the nature of an accident. Under the guidance of Mr. C. K. T. Naidoo, they made Newcastle their headquarters, and, travelling from mine to mine, they made eloquent appeal to the Indian labourers and their families to cease work until an assurance of repeal of the tax was given by the Government. The response was immediate and general. Mine after mine was closed down, as the Indian labourers refused to work, and a state of panic ensued amongst the employers, who at first continued to give rations as an inducement to their employees to remain on the mines. A hurried conference of mine-owners was held at Durban, at which Mr. Gandhi was invited to be present, and he then explained the situation and referred to the promise made to Mr. Gokhale. He pointed out that the labourers were being asked to strike only so long as the £3 Tax was unrepealed, and because it had been alleged—an allegation that was subsequently discovered to be well-founded—that the employers were opposed to repeal. The conference telegraphed to General Smuts inquiring about the promise, which was denied by him and by General Botha, for the first time; but it is significant that the late Mr. Fischer, who was also present at the meeting with the Ministers, did not repudiate it, though his physical condition did not preclude his doing so. Mr. Gokhale at once cabled, stating that a promise of repeal had undoubtedly been made to him, and, as a result of the hostile attitude now taken up by the Government and by the employers, the labourers were invited to leave the mines, where improper influences were being used to induce them to return to work.

Mr. Gandhi placed himself at the head of a vast commissariat organisation, and, together with a small body of assistants, chief of whom was Mr. Albert Christopher, and with the co-operation of Mr. Kallenbach, the Indians—men, women and children—were fed and maintained at Newcastle, where they flocked by the hundred, coming by road and rail as fast as they could leave the mines, with the result that the latter, from Dundee and Ladysmith to Newcastle, were denuded of their labour supply. It was a pathetic and yet a cheering sight to watch these patient hundreds plodding slowly along muddy roads, in inclement weather, to the Newcastle centre, where they lived on a handful of rice, bread, and sugar a day, in the open, without shelter, without cooking accommodation beyond what they improvised on the bare veld, without comfort of any kind. But they were buoyed up with a great hope, and they had an inspiring leader. Mr. Kallenbach, too, fought their battles for them with the Newcastle municipality and magistracy, and later they saw how Mr. Gandhi shared their daily life and hardships, nursed the sick, and fed the hungry. They knew that the Indian women, who had urged them to strike, were cheerfully suffering imprisonment with hard labour, for their sake, and they felt in honour bound to struggle on until they had secured the repeal of the tax that weighed so heavily upon so many of them. And the women amongst them were no less heroic than the men. One mother, whose little child died of exposure on the road to Newcastle, was heard to say: "We must not pine for the dead; it is the living for which we must work." Such a spirit ensured ultimate success.

As their members swelled, it was felt that the only possible method of compelling the Union Government to realise their responsibilities and assume charge was to march the whole of the strikers into the Transvaal, there to court arrest and imprisonment, and it was accordingly decided to concentrate at Charlestown, the border village, where Messrs. Vallibhai and Mukdoom rendered great service. At the head of a large "army," therefore, Mr. Gandhi marched there on October 30th, but just before the march commenced, a number of strikers were arrested and removed to the gaols after sentence of imprisonment. Day by day hundreds more marched to or entrained for Charlestown, where a vast camp was organised, under the sanitary control of the District Health Officer, Dr. Briscoe, and rations, that were pouring in from Durban and Johannesburg Indian merchants, to which were added supplies purchased with money that was being cabled in large sums from India, were daily distributed to a gathering of men, women and children that numbered finally over 3,000.

Meanwhile, Mr. Gandhi had telegraphed the intentions of the "invaders" to the Government, who apparently took no notice of the warning. Simultaneously, efforts were made, without success, by the Deputy Protector to induce the strikers to return to work, and large batches of them were arrested, and eventually imprisoned.

At last, a week after the notification, Mr. Gandhi commenced the now famous "invasion" of the Transvaal, with a following of over 2,000. The women and children were left behind at Charlestown, in charge of Miss

Schlesin and Mr. Kallenbach, who worked day and night to make their lot somewhat easier. At the border, the "army" came to a stand, whilst Mr. Gandhi, who was near the rear, having remained behind to make final arrangements, came forward to interview the police officer who, with a small patrol, was on duty at the gate of entry. Whilst these preliminaries were in train, the main body became impatient, and a mass of cheering, shouting Indians, clad in ragged clothes, and bearing their pitifully small belongings upon their heads, swarmed through the streets of Volksrust, determined to do or die, brushing the handful of police aside like so many helpless and insignificant atoms. They encamped on the farther side of the town, and the great march had commenced. The programme was to march, at the rate of some 25 miles a day, until the men were arrested, or Tolstoy Farm, at Lawley, near Johannesburg, was reached, and the Government were informed of each stopping-place. Eight days were set aside to reach their destination, unless they were earlier arrested, and, from the swing and energy of their marching, it was plain that a phenomenal feat was being performed by men, many of them heavily burdened, unused to conditions of "war," but accustomed to hard and simple life, and on a meagre and unusual diet. That night they reached Palmford, where special accommodation was offered to Mr. Gandhi, who, however, refused to accept hospitality which his humbler countrymen could not share.

Meanwhile, the Government were not altogether idle, but with that stupidity which almost invariably characterises governments in similiar emergencies, they did the wrong thing, and issued a warrant for the arrest of Mr. Gandhi, hoping thus to demoralise the forces that he was leading. Mr. Gandhi surrendered to the warrant of Palmford, having, at the request of the authorities, pointed out some of his own followers to give evidence for him, as the Crown would not otherwise have been able to prove its case against him! He was motored swiftly to Volksrust, but the "army" silently and grimly pursued its march undeterred by the loss of its revered leader. At Volksrust, Mr. Gandhi was charged with breach of the Immigration Act and applied for bail, as he was in charge of large numbers of men entirely dependent upon him, and his application was granted. Realising, however, the probable risks that would ensue if the people were left leaderless, he addressed the following telegram to the Minister of the Interior:

"Whilst I appreciate the fact of Government having at last arrested prime mover in passive resistance struggle, cannot help remarking that from point view humanity moment chosen most unfortunate. Government probably know that marchers include 122 women, 50 tender children, all voluntarily marching on starvation rations without provision for shelter during stages. Tearing me away under such circumstances from them is violation all considerations justice. When arrested last night, left men without informing them. They might become infuriated. I, therefore, ask either that I may be allowed continue march with men, or Government send them by rail Tolstoy Farm and provide full rations for them. Leaving them without one in whom they have confidence, and without Government making provision for them, is, in my opinion, an act from which I hope on reconsideration Government will recoil. If untoward incidents happen during further progress march, or if deaths occur, especially amongst women with babies in arms, responsibility will be Government's." No reply was returned to this humane appeal, but it was understood that the Government had no intention of assuming charge of this large body of men, women and children. Writing at the time of Mr. Gandhi's arrest, the special correspondent of the *Natal Mercury* sent his paper the following vivid description of the conditions prevailing both then and earlier at Charlestown :—

"We arrived at Palmford about 8-30 P.M. last night, and found them all sleeping in the veld, just below the station. Many of them were feeling the cold severely . . . I visited Charlestown twice on the 5th (the day before the march commenced). The whole appearance of the town resembled nothing but an Indian bazaar. The town was crowded with Indians . . . No sanitary arrangements were made at first, and the position from a health point of view was awful; but later Mr. Gandhi assisted the municipal officials, and the position was greatly improved. I found Mr. Gandhi at the back of an Indian store, in the yard, serving out curry and rice to his followers, who marched up, and each man received his quota. One baker sold 5,000 loaves to the Indians in one day."

Mr. Gandhi, upon his release on bail, swiftly motored back to his followers, rejoining them on the march, which proceeded quietly as far as Paardeberg, where the remaining women and children were left behind in charge of a few of the men, who had become footsore. The main body reached Standerton on the morning of the 8th, where a number of strikers were arrested by their compound managers, assisted by a few police, and entrained for Natal. And here, too, Mr. Gandhi was re-arrested on the same charge as before. He again requested bail, and, owing to the attitude of the strikers, who persistently refused to move from the Court precincts until their leader was restored to them, his request was granted, and the march was resumed immediately.

Sunday, the 9th, was an historic day. With a view to a final consultation with him before leaving for India, Mr. Polak had telegraphed to Mr. Gandhi, saying that he was joining him, and had received a wire suggesting Greylingstad as the meeting place, but with the warning that he (Mr. Polak) might be arrested if he came. He joined the column at a small place named Teakworth, a few miles on the Standerton side of Greylingstad. The "army," spread along the road for a distance of some three miles, was led by a small, limping, bent, but dogged man, coarsely dressed, and using a staff, with a serene and peaceful countenance, however, and a look of sureness and content. That was Gandhi, the principal Passive Resister. The two friends greeted each other, and eagerly exchanged news. Whilst thus engaged, and when about an hour distant from Greylingstad, not far ahead was seen a Cape cart, and walking rapidly towards them were a couple of police officers, behind whom came Mr. M. Chamney, the Principal Immigration Officer of the Transvaal. Realising the pacific nature of the demonstration and of the Indian leader's intentions, Mr. Chamney had complimented Mr. Gandhi by undertaking his arrest upon a warrant issued under the Natal Indenture Law with no stronger support than this. The Cape cart, with its precious freight, drove swiftly away, and the column resumed its march quietly, under the leadership of Mr. Polak, who had at once assumed the responsibility, preceded by the two mounted policemen. A few minutes later, Messrs. Cachalia and Bhyat, who, together with Mr. Badat of Volksrust, were in charge of the commissariat arrangements, of which Mr. Polak was in entire ignorance, joined the column, having accidentally missed it in on another road, and they at once proceeded to Balfour, where it was due next morning and where food supplies were awaiting its arrival. The evening was fine and clear, and the cooking-fires that were lit from end to end of the veldt offered a bright and sparkling spectacle. Gradually, the buzz and throb of conversation sank, as sleep fell upon the camp. The night, however, was dismal and wretched, a cold wind howled mournfully down from the neighbouring hills, and a drizzle of rain added to the discomfort of the shelterless throng.

But the night was portentous, for it was decreed that the march should end on the morrow, though of this the marchers were as yet unware. At four in the morning it was resumed, and the moving mass of heroic men swung forward into their stride, covering the ground at a splendid pace, and, laden as they were, without waggons and without food, they travelled the distance between Greylingstad and Balfour, 13 miles, in 3½ hours. Upon reaching the latter place, without any police escort, just before 9 a.m., it became evident that the last stage had been reached, for three special trains were drawn up at the station to take back the strikers to Natal. Mr. Polak was approached by the Police Officer in charge of the arrangements, and by Mr. Chamney, to co-operate with them in effecting the arrest of the "army," and upon receiving their assurance that the men were really to be sent to Natal, where criminal proceedings were awaiting them, he replied that he would gladly do so as the whole object of the march had thus been fulfilled, and his own responsibility ceased. At the same time, he offered himself for arrest also, but he was informed that the Government did not desire this. He, however, warned the officials that, in Mr. Gandhi's enforced absence, it might be difficult for him to induce compliance with their desire, as but few of the men had ever seen him before. Mr. Gandhi, however, was passing through from Heideberg, en route for Dundee, where he was subsequently imprisoned, and sent a message urging the people quietly to surrender.

They were fed as rapidly as food could be supplied to them—a handful of rice and bread each—and then Mr. Chamney, having questioned them as to their proofs of rights of residence, proclaimed them prohibited immigrants. For the moment, chaos prevailed, as a number of stalwarts, who had set their hearts upon reaching Johannesburg, called upon the multitude to march forward, but, instantly realising the danger of this movement, which, whilst it would have resulted in bloodshed, would have swept aside the small band of twenty-five policemen in the twinkling of an eye, and let loose an uncontrolled body of men to roam over the Transvaal, who would not afterwards probably have been located. Mr. Polak, followed by Messrs. Cachalia and Bhyat, rushed to the head of the column and implored the people to remember that their object, as passive resisters, was not Johannesburg but gaol, and eventually peace was restored. Gradually, and in small groups, the men entrained, Mr. Polak accompanying the first train as far as Charlestown, where he was shortly afterwards arrested. Here, the strikers having been locked up without food or water for eight hours, the trains were not allowed to remain more than a couple of minutes, the platform being occupied by armed police, who kept back the women that had remained there and now urged their menfolk, with tears in their eyes and choking voices, not to mind them but to remain true to their duty. And slowly the trains steamed south, bearing nearly two thousand humble heroes to a bitter fate and a shameful experience, but firm in the knowledge that they had done what they had set out to do, and that the repeal of the hated tax was now certain. The great and impressive march was over.

The *Times* has since declared that it must live in memory as one of the most remarkable manifestations in history of the spirit of Passive Resistance. It had achieved all that its organisers, in their fondest dreams, had hoped for it. It had proclaimed, as nothing else could have done, the stubborn endurance, the dogged persistency, the grim tenacity, the stern determination, the magnificent self-sacrifice of the Passive Resisters. And it assured success. It was not a defeat, as the shallow critics had at the time proclaimed it. Had the strikers not exercised, under the guidance of trusted leaders, immense self-control—there was no pillage, no disorder, no violence—all the forces that the Government had brought against them could not have prevented their swarming over the Transvaal. But it was the glorious ending of a peaceful demonstration of workers determined upon achieving freedom for themselves, their wives, their children. A splendid victory for Truth had been won. The honour of the Indian Motherland had been vindicated. Mr. Gokhale's word had been made good.

And the sign of this is to be found in the work of Messrs. Andrews and Pearson, the report of the Commission, its acceptance by the Government, the debates in Parliament, and the passing of Act 22 of 1914, repealing the £3 Tax for ever and granting freedom of residence in Natal to those who choose to remain unindentured. The real victory is that of the soul-force of the marchers, starving, weary, but buoyed up with unconquerable hope, over the brute-force of those who had declared their intention at all costs to maintain them in a condition of perpetual helotage."

Thus ended the great march. The majesty of the law was once more vindicated by the arrest, trial and imprisonment of thousands. Mr. Gandhi himself who, as the account quoted above mentions, had been arrested at Volksrust and released on bail was subsequently tried and sentenced to fifteen months. At the trial he delivered himself as follows:—

Addressing the Court at Volksrust, Mr. Gandhi said that he had given the Minister of the Interior due notice of his intention to cross the border with the prohibited immigrants, and had informed the Immigration Officer at Volksrust of the date of crossing. He assured the Court that the present movement had nothing whatever to do with the unlawful entry of a single Indian for the purpose of residence in the Transvaal. He might fairly claim that during his whole career in the Transvaal he had been actuated by a desire to assist the Government in preventing surreptitious entry and unlawful settlement, but he pleaded guilty to knowingly committing an offence against the Section under which he was charged. He was aware that his action was fraught with the greatest risks and intense personal suffering to his followers. He was convinced that nothing short of much suffering would move the conscience of the Governor, or of the inhabitants of the Union, of which, in spite of this breach of the laws, he claimed to be a sane and law-abiding citizen.

The strike on the coal-mines had meanwhile spread to the sugar plantations in Natal. A savage attempt was made to suppress it and in the attempt some of the strikers were shot dead, and several injured.

The cup of suffering was now full to the brim. Resentment in India had reached white heat. The Government of India were alarmed at the situation. And Lord Hardinge then Viceroy of India, in his famous speech at Madras, placed himself at the head of Indian public opinion and asked for the appointment of a commission to institute a searching enquiry into the whole matter. The Imperial Authorities also bestirred themselves as they had never done before. And the authors of the policy which had led to such incalculable misery and bitterness now for the first time showed likewise unmistakable signs of relenting by acceding to the demand for the commission of enquiry. But when it was actually constituted with Sir William Solomon as President, its composition rendered it so dubious that the Indian leaders resolved to ignore it altogether. It was at this crisis of affairs that the well-known missionary gentlemen, the Rev. Messrs. Andrews and Pearson, true children of the Man of Sorrows paid a visit to South Africa and by their persistent endeavours in influential circles were able to diffuse a healing spirit. All is well that ends well. The findings of the Solomon commission were favourable to the Indian community on all points referred to it for report. Its recommendations were endorsed without reservation by the Union Government and given effect to by the subsequent passing of the Indians' Relief Act. This gave satisfaction to the Indian Community and Mr. Gandhi formally announced the closing of the struggle.

It will be interesting at this stage to take stock of the results achieved by the concentrated suffering of eight long years. But we shall miss its significance if we do not grasp clearly at the outset that the battle was from first to last a moral and spiritual one, and was waged not for the compassing of material ends but for the vindication of manhood. And from this point of view it surely realised its purpose in a measure that the great protagonists of the movement themselves could not at first have dreamed of. The struggle was the means, the struggle was the end. To those who have known the intensity of aspiration and elevation of character that made the fight possible the talk of material results must ever seem a pitiful meanness. Such have received the initiation of the highest self-knowledge. They have been face to face with that mood of the soul which sights nothing but endless horizons of spiritual endeavour and achievement. They have known that the life of the ordinary selfish man is not the real life but that deep within everyone high or low sleeps a heaven into which some day we shall all awake.

Furthermore they have created for their children and their children's children the priceless memory of a heroic past. And down to the remotest generations will linger the pride of how the forefathers braved the fury of the persecutor and staked their all for nothing but their own honour. Nay shall not the motherland herself treasure for ever the story of the deeds of the humblest of her children in a far away land as it has treasured the legend of Rama and Sita, or that of the Pandava brothers? Will not humanity itself the world over feel a quickened sense of its own divinity as it peruses the same golden record? Has not another chapter been added to the world's Acts of the Apostles?

Let us now reckon the tale of the martyrs to whom it was given to give their lives to the cause. There was that young girl, Valiamma of whom Mr. Gandhi has said: "Simple-minded in faith she had not the knowledge that he had, she did not know what passive resistance was, she did not know what it was the community would gain, but she was simply taken up with unbounded enthusiasm for her people—went to gaol, came out of it a wreck, and within a few days died." There were the two youths from the Tamil land, Nagappan and Narayanaswamy—the former died shortly after his release from prison, and the latter at Delgoa Bay after having vainly attempted to land in South Africa as already told. And lastly there was the old man Harbatsingh, a Hindustani stalwart who went to gaol as a passive resister when he was seventy-five, and who when questioned by Mr. Gandhi why he had come, had answered. "What does it matter? I know what you are fighting for. You have not to pay the £3 tax

MISS VALIAMMA

Who died after serving a term of imprisonment as a Passive Resister.

MRS. SHEIK MEATAB,

An Indian Mahomedan Woman Passive Resister.

but my fellow ex-indentured Indians have to pay that tax, and what more glorious death could I meet?" And he met his death in the gaol at Durban.

Coming lower down the scale, the feeling of contempt for the 'coloured man' which had so long possessed the white settlers has yielded place to one of respect and admiration. The instinct of race-superiority has been knocked out of at least the better mind of the Union. The principle of differentiation on racial grounds has disappeared. The livery of manhood shines in place of the badge of servitude. Unfading lustre has been reflected upon the name of the mother-country, and an invaluable contribution made to the life of Indian Nationalism.

And last but not least, the struggle has removed the mask from the small emaciated figure known to the world as Mohandas Karamchand Gandhi, and set him before the world in his true lineaments—a moral giant, a spiritual hero, and a peerless soldier of God.

The material fruits of the struggle were in themselves by no means inconsiderable. The hated law which started the whole trouble was repealed. The £3 tax has been abolished.

The recognition of Indian marriages has been secured. The system of indentured immigration has been put an end to. And most important of all, the passing of further laws intended to drive out the Indians from South Africa, which would certainly have followed, was nipped in the bud. But of none of these gains could it be said that it was wholly material.

There are still great disabilities under which the Indian resident of the Union has to labour. These we shall enumerate in the words of Mr. Gandhi himself: "There was still the gold law which had many a sting in it. There was still the Licensing laws throughout the Union which also contained many a sting. There was still a matter which the colonial-born Indians could not understand or appreciate, namely, the water-tight compartments in which they had to live; whilst there was free inter-communication and inter-migration between the provinces for the Europeans, Indians had to be cooped up in their respective provinces. Then there was undue restraint on their trading activity. There was the prohibition as to their holding landed property in the Transvaal which was degrading and all these things took Indians into all sorts of undesirable channels." Further the Indians have yet to be admitted to the political franchise. The sympathy which takes an equal interest in all classes of the ruled is still far distant. And lastly the practical stoppage of immigration from India has deprived the South African Indians of that opportunity of living intercourse with the mother country which he cannot but value so highly. These and like wrongs will have to be set right in the future, God grant without the necessity of similar struggles!

The sense of truimph and rejoicing which marked the closing of the memorable struggle was mingled by the sadness of the thought that the great central figure, the genius and inspirer of the whole movement, the redeemer and Avatar of the Indian community in South Africa was soon to depart to the motherland for ever. Heightened a thousandfold was the pathos of farewell which in this case is best left to the imagination. His mission accomplished, the conquering hero returned to his native land in the faith, as he has said, that "it is in India that the nearest approach to perfection is most possible."

The welcome accorded to Mr. Gandhi on his return home, was characterised by all the warmth, affection, and delicate reverence which India alone of all lands knows to offer to the great of soul. Since his return to this country he has been mainly devoting himself to a personal study and comprehension of the problems with which a great and ancient civilisation in process of transition to a new order necessarily teems. For this purpose, he has been going about from place to place, making the acquaintance of people of all grades and conditions, and coming into contact with the leaders of thought and activity. A man's character is written in his slightest acts and when during the early days of his arrival in this country, he was seen alighting from a third class compartment, at Howrah station, while the elite of Calcutta, assembled on the platform, were making a search for him in the first and second-class compartments, almost a sensation was caused. This was no vanity of humility on his part but proceeded from the firm resolve not to stain himself by any luxury which is not accessible to the poorest in the land. It was simply that passionate determination to one himself with the sorrows of the lowest and meanest of which his daily life is so eloquent an expression. And recently, he has become the fiery champion of the woes of the third-class passenger! In his eyes there is no wrong so trivial as to be unworthy of his earnest attention and striving. Such is the spirit that he has brought to the task of nation-making in this land.

There was again that incident at the opening of the Hindu University, when the platform was crowded with Rajahs and Maharajahs, and Mr. Gandhi made a speech at which several people left the meeting construing his words to be disloyal. It was sheer misunderstanding, as it afterwards turned out, of the spirit of a man whose whole life is a consuming effort to throw out of himself the very seed of hatred and every slightest motion of mind or heart which could have the shadow of any reaction of evil.

The Champaran incident is still fresh in the mind of the public and requires no elaboration. He had gone there on invitation to undertake an enquiry as to the conditions of the labourers in the Indigo plantations and the treatment meted out to them by their employers. The District Magistrate of Champaran took it into his head that his presence was a serious danger to the district and would lead to a breach of the peace. And he had an order served upon Mr. Gandhi to the effect that the latter was to leave the district by the 'next available train.' Mr. Gandhi replied that he had come there out of a sense of duty and would stay and submit to the penalty of disobedience. At the trial that followed he simply pleaded guilty, and made a statement that he was faced by a conflict of duty, the duty of obeying the law and the duty of enquiry upon which he had come, and that under the circumstances he could only throw the responsibility of removing him on the administration. The Magistrate postponed judgment till some hours later in the day, and at the interview with the District Magistrate the same day he undertook not to go out to the village till instructions were received from the provincial administration. The case was adjourned to some days later, and the higher authorities subsequently issued instructions not to proceed with the prosecution. Some of the planters took the occasion to make a rabid attack upon Mr. Gandhi, but the recently published report of the Champaran commission of enquiry which was the immediate result of his visit has amply justified him.

The idea of a monster petition to the authorities from the people is not new in the modern political history of India. But when Mr. Gandhi revived the suggestion in connection with the Congress-Moslem-League scheme of reform, the moment was most opportune and the idea caught like magic. He himself undertook the propaganda in his own province of Gujarat and carried it out with characteristic thoroughness. The true patriot can never be idle, neither can he ever rest on his oars.

But far the most pregnant act of his in India has been the establishment of the *Satyagrahasrama*. As its name signifies, it stands for truth, truth as the highest consideration of all, truth in thought, word and deed. Its members have likewise to take the vow of celibacy, the vow of control of the palate, the vow of non-thieving, the vow of Swadeshi, the vow of fearlessness, and the vow of redeeming the untouchables in India. That education should be imparted through the vernaculars is also one of its cardinal principles. The Ashrama is thus the nucleus of a great new order for the perfecting of the individual and the uplifting of the nation.

It is as the embodiment of *Satyagraha*, as a veritable lamp burning upon the altar, that Mohandas Karamchand Gandhi stands to-day before his countrymen. Truth-force or love-force, as he himself has translated the term into English, is to him the greatest of all powers. In proportion as individuals and nations alike fulfil the law of this power and fit themselves into it they live and grow: the rest is death. The delicacy of insight and vision, the force of character, and all the virtues which have thrown a mantle of splendour over his name are but the fruit of this central realisation carried into action. It would be vain to speculate as to what he would have become had his life been cast in other places than South Africa. God sends his chosen servants to do the work appointed for them. It is ours to recognize them.

SPEECHES AND WRITINGS

OF

M. K. GANDHI

GANDHI'S SENSE OF DUTY

[*The following exhortation was addressed by Mr. M. K. Gandhi to the Tamil community of South Africa*] :—

Remember that we are descendants, of Prahlad and Sudhanva, both passive resisters of the purest type. They disregarded the dictates even of their parents, when they were asked to deny God. They suffered extreme torture rather than inflict suffering on their persecutors. We in the Transvaal are being called upon to deny God, in that we are required to deny our manhood, go back upon our oath, and accept an insult to our nation. Shall we, in the present crisis, do less than our fore-fathers ?

GANDHI'S CONFESSION OF FAITH

[*The following is an extract from a letter addressed by Mr. Gandhi to a friend in India*] :—

(1) There is no impassable barrier between East and West.

(2) There is no such thing as Western or European civilization but there is a modern civilization, which is purely material.

(3) The people of Europe, before they were touched by modern civilization had much in common with the people of the East; anyhow the people of India, and even to-day Europeans who are not touched by Modern civilization are far better able to mix with Indians than the offspring of that civilization.

(4) It is not the British people who are ruling India, but it is modern civilisation, through its railways, telegraph, telephone, and almost every invention which has been claimed to be a triumph of civilization.

(5) Bombay, Calcutta, and the other chief cities of India are the real Plague spots.

(6) If British rule was replaced to-morrow by Indian rule based on modern methods, India would be no better, except that she would be able then to retain some of the money that is drained away to England; but then India would only become a second or fifth edition of Europe or America.

(7) East and West can only and really meet when the West has thrown overboard modern civilization, almost in its entirety. They can also seemingly meet when East has also adopted modern civilization, but that meeting would be an armed truce, even as it is between, say, Germany and England, both of which nations are living in the Hall of Death in order to avoid being devoured the one by the other.

(8) It is simply impertinence for any man or any body of men to begin or contemplate reform of the whole world. To attempt to do so by means of highly artificial and speedy locomotion, is to attempt the impossible.

(9) Increase of material comforts, it may be generally laid down, does not in any way whatsoever conduce to moral growth.

(10) Medical Science is the concentrated essence of Black Magic. Quackery is infinitely

preferable to what passes for high medical skill.

(11) Hospitals are the instruments that the Devil has been using for his own purpose, in order to keep his hold on his Kingdom. They perpetuate vice, misery, and degradation and real slavery. I was entirely off the track when I considered that I should receive a medical training. It would be sinful for me in any way whatsoever to take part in the abominations that go on in the hospitals. If there were no hospitals for venereal diseases, or even for consumptives, we should have less consumption, and less sexual vice amongst us.

(12) India's salvation consists in unlearning what she has learnt during the past fifty years. The railways, telegraphs, hospitals, lawyers, doctors, and such like have all to go, and the so-called upper classes have to learn to live consciously and religiously and deliberately the simple peasant life, knowing it to be a life-giving, true happiness.

(13) India should wear no machine-made clothing, whether it comes out of European mills or Indian mills.

(14) England can help India to do this, and then she will have justified her hold on India.

There seem to be many in England to-day who think likewise.

(15) There was true wisdom in the sages of old having so regulated society as to limit the material condition of the people; the rude plough of perhaps five thousand years ago is the plough of the husbandman to-day. Therein lies salvation. People live long under such conditions, in comparative peace much greater than Europe has enjoyed after having taken up modern activity, and I feel that every enlightened man, certainly every Englishman, may, if he chooses learn this truth and act according to it.

It is the true spirit of passive resistance that has brought me to the above almost definite conclusions. As a passive resister, I am unconcerned whether such a gigantic, reformation, shall I call it, can be brought about among people who find their satisfaction from the present mad rush. If I realize the truth of it, I should rejoice in following it, and therefore I could not wait until the whole body of people had commenced. All of us who think likewise have to take the necessary step, and the rest, if we are in the right, must follow. The theory is there: our practice will have to approach it as much as possible. Living in the midst of the rush, we may not be able to shake ourselves free from all taint. Every time I get into a railway car or use a motor-bus, I know that I am doing violence to my sense of what is right. I do not fear the logical result on that basis. The visiting of England is bad, and any communication between South Africa and India by means of ocean-grey-hounds is also bad, and so on. You and I can, and may outgrow these things in our present bodies, but the chief thing is to put our theory right. You will be seeing there all sorts and conditions of men. I therefore feel that I should no longer withold from you what I call the progressive step I have taken mentally. If you agree with me, then it will be your duty to tell the revolutionaries and every body else that the freedom they want, or they think they want, is not to be obtained by killing people or doing violence, but by setting themselves right, and by becoming and remaining truly Indian. Then the British rulers will be servants and not masters. They will be trustees, and not tyrants, and they will live in perfect peace with the whole of the inhabitants of India. The future, therefore, lies not with the British race, but with the Indians themselves, and if they have sufficient self-abnegation and abstemiousness, they can make themselves free this very moment, and when we have arrived in India at the simplicity which is still ours largely and which was ours entirely until a few years ago, it will still be possible for the best Indians and the best Europeans to see one another throughout the length and breadth of India, and act as the leaven. When there was no rapid locomotion, teachers and preachers went on foot, from one end of the country to the other, braving all dangers, not for pleasure, not for recruiting their health, (though all that followed from their tramps) but for the sake of humanity. Then were Benares and other places of pilgrimage holy cities, whereas to-day they are an abomination.

You will recollect you used to hate me for talking to my children in Guzerati. I now feel more and more convinced that I was absolutely right in refusing to talk to them in English. Fancy a Guzerati writing to another Guzerati in English! Which, as you would properly say, he mispronounces, and writes ungrammatically. I should certainly never commit the ludicrous blunders in writing in Guzerati that I do in writing or speaking in English. I think that when I speak in English to an Indian or a Foreigner I in a measure un-learn the language. If I want to learn it well, and if I want to attune my ear to it, I can only do so by talking to an Englishman and by listening to an Englishman speaking.

GANDHI'S PLEA FOR THE SOUL

[*The following is an extract from a letter of the London correspondent of the Amrita Bazar Patrika, summarising an address delivered by Mr. Gandhi before the members of the Emerson Club and of the Hampstead Branch of the Peace and Arbitration Society whilst in London*] :—

Mr. Gandhi turned to India, and spoke with enthusiasm of Rama, the victim of the machinations of a woman choosing fourteen years' exile rather than surrender; other Orientals were mentioned, and then, through the Doukhabors of to-day, he brought the thoughts of the audience to the soul resistance of Indians *versus* brute force in South Africa. He insisted that it was completely a mistake to believe that Indians were incapable of lengthened resistance for a principle; in their fearlessness of suffering they were second to none in the world. Passive resistance had been called a weapon of the weak, but Mr. Gandhi maintained that it required courage higher than that of a soldier on the battle-field, which was often the impulse of the moment, for passive resistance, was continuous and sustained; it meant physical suffering. Some people were inclined to think it too difficult to be carried out to-day, but those who held that idea were not moved by true courage. Again referring to Oriental teaching, Mr. Gandhi said that the teaching of the "Lord's Song" was, from the beginning, the necessity of fearlessness. He touched on the question of physical force while insisting that it was not thought of by Indians in the Transvaal. He does not want to share in liberty for India that is gained by violence and bloodshed, and insists that no country is so capable as India of wielding soul force. Mr. Gandhi did not approve of the militant tactics of the suffragates for the reason that they were meeting body force with body force, and not using the higher power of soul force; violence begot violence. He maintained, too, that the association of Britain and India must be a mutual benefit if India—eschewing violence—did not depart from her proud position of being the giver and the teacher of religion. "If the world believes in the existence of the soul," he said in conclusion, "it must be recognised that soul force is better than body force: it is the sacred principle of love which moves mountains. To us is the responsibility of living out this sacred law; we are not concerned with results."

Mr. Gandhi protested against the mad rush of to-day and, instead of blessing the means by which modern science has made this mad rush possible, that is, railways, motors, telegraph, telephone, and even the coming flying machines, he declared that they were diverting man's thoughts from the main purpose of life; bodily comfort stood before soul growth; man had no time to-day even to know himself; he preferred a newspaper or sport or other things rather than to be left alone with himself for thought. He claimed Ruskin as on his side in this expression to protest against the drive and hurry of modern civilisation. He did not describe this development of material science as exclusively British, but he considered that its effect in India had been baneful in many ways. He instanced the desecration of India's holy places, which he said were no longer holy for the "fatal facility" of locomotion had brought to those places people whose only aim was to defraud the unsophisticated; such people in the olden days when pilgrimages meant long and wearisome walking through jungles, crossing rivers, and encountering many dangers, had not the stamina to reach the goal. Pilgrimages in those days could only be undertaken by the cream of society, but they came to know each other; the aim of the holy places was to make India holy. Plague and famine, which existed in pre-British days were local then; to-day, locomotion had caused them to spread. To avoid the calamity which intense materialism must bring, Mr. Gandhi urged that India should go back to her former holiness, which is not yet lost. The contact with the West has awakened her from the lethargy into which she had sunk; the new spirit, if properly directed, would bring blessings to both nations and to the world. If India adopted Western modern civilisation as Japan had done, there must be perpetual conflict and gasping between Briton and Indian. If, on the other hand, India's ancient civilisation can withstand this latest assault, as it has withstood so many before, and be, as of old, the religious teacher, the spiritual guide, then there would be no impassable barrier between East and West. Some circumstances exist, said Mr. Gandhi, which we cannot understand; but the main purpose of life is to live rightly, think rightly, act rightly; but the soul must languish when we give all our thought to the body.

THE DUTIES OF BRITISH CITIZENSHIP

I consider myself a lover of the British Empire, a citizen (though voteless) of the Transvaal, prepared to take my full share in promoting the general well-being of the country. And I claim it to be perfectly honourable and consistent with the above profession to advise my countrymen not to submit to the Asiatic Act, as being derogatory to their manhood and offensive to their religion. And I claim, too, that the method of passive resistance adopted to combat the mischief is the clearest and safest, because, if the cause is not true, it is the resisters, and they alone who suffer. I am perfectly aware of the danger to good government, in a country inhabited by many races unequally developed, in an honest citizen advising resistance to a law of the land. But I refuse to believe in the infallibility of legislators, I do believe that they are not always guided by generous or even just sentiments in their dealings with unrepresented classes. I venture to say that, if passive resistance is generally accepted, it will once and for ever avoid the contingency of a terrible death-struggle and bloodshed in the event (not impossible) of the natives being exasperated by a stupid mistake of our legislators.

It has been said that those who do not like the law may leave the country. This is all very well spoken from a cushioned chair, but it is neither possible nor becoming for men to leave their homes because they do not subscribe to certain laws enacted against them. The inlanders of the Boer regime complained of harsh laws; they, too, were told that if they did not like them they could retire from the country. Are Indians, who are fighting for their self-respect, to slink away from the country for fear of suffering imprisonment or worse? If I could help it, nothing would remove Indians from the country save brute force. It is no part of a citizen's duty to pay blind obedience to the laws imposed on him. And if my countrymen believe in God and the existence of the soul, then, while they may admit that their bodies belong to the state to be imprisoned and deported, their minds, their wills, and their souls must ever remain free like the birds of the air, and are beyond the reach of the swiftest arrow.—(*Indian Opinion*).

THE THEORY AND PRACTICE OF PASSIVE RESISTANCE

[*The following is reproduced from the Golden Number of the Indian Opinion*, 1914] :—

I shall be at least far away from Phœnix, if not actually in the Motherland, when this Commemoration Issue is published. I would, however, leave behind me my innermost thoughts upon that which has made this special issue necessary. Without Passive Resistance, there would have been no richly illustrated and important special issue of *Indian Opinion*, which has, for the last eleven years, in an unpretentious and humble manner, endeavoured to serve my countrymen and South Africa, a period covering the most critical stage that they will perhaps ever have to pass through. It marks the rise and growth of Passive Resistance, which has attracted world-wide attention. The term does not fit the activity of the Indian community during the past eight years. Its equivalent in the vernacular, rendered into English, means

Truth-Force. I think Tolstoy called it also Soul-Force or Love-Force, and so it is. Carried out to its utmost limit, this force is independent of pecuniary or other material assistance; certainly, even in its elementary form, of physical force or violence. Indeed, violence is the negation of this great spiritual force, which can only be cultivated or wielded by those who will entirely eschew violence. It is force that may be used by individuals as well as by communities. It may be used as well in political as in domestic affairs. Its universal applicability is a demonstration of its permanence an invincibility. It can be used alike by men, women, and children. It is totally untrue to say that it is a force to be used only by the weak so long as they are not capable of meeting violence by violence. This superstition arises from the incompleteness of the English expression. It is impossible for those who consider themselves to be weak to apply this force. Only those who realise that there is something in man which is superior to the brute nature in him, and that the latter always yields to it, can effectively be Passive Resisters. This force is to violence and, therefore, to all tyranny, all injustice, what light is to darkness. In politics, its use is based upon the immutable maxim that government of the people is possible only so long as they consent either consciously or unconsciously to be governed. We did not want to be governed by the Asiatic Act of 1907 of the Transvaal, and it had to go before this mighty force. Two courses were open to us—to use violence when we were called upon to submit to the Act, or to suffer the penalties prescribed under the Act, and thus to draw out and exhibit the force of the soul within us for a period long enough to appeal to the sympathetic chord in the governors or the law-makers. We have taken long to achieve what we set about striving for. That was because our Passive Resistance was not of the most complete type. All Passive Resisters do not understand the full value of the force, nor have we men who always from conviction refrain from violence. The use of this force requires the adoption of poverty, in the sense that we must be indifferent whether we have the wherewithal to feed or clothe ourselves. During the past struggle, all Passive Resisters, if any at all, were not prepared to go that length. Some again were only Passive Resisters so-called. They came without any conviction, often with mixed motives, less often with impure motives. Some even, whilst engaged in the struggle, would gladly have resorted to violence but for most vigilant supervision. Thus it was that the struggle became prolonged; for the exercise of the purest soul-force, in its perfect form, brings about instantaneous relief. For this exercise, prolonged training of the individual soul is an absolute necessity, so that a perfect Passive Resister has to be almost, if not entirely, a perfect man. We cannot all suddenly become such men, but, if my proposition is correct—as I know it to be correct—the greater the spirit of Passive Resistance in us, the better men we will become. Its use, therefore, is, I think, indisputable, and it is a force which, if it became universal, would revolutionise social ideals and do away with despotisms and the ever-growing militarism under which the nations of the West are groaning and are being almost crushed to death, and which fairly promises to overwhelm even the nations of the East. If the past struggle has produced even a few Indians who would dedicate themselves to the task of becoming Passive Resisters as nearly perfect as possible, they would not only have served themselves in the truest sense of the term, they would also have served humanity at large. Thus viewed, Passive Resistance is the noblest and the best education. It should come, not after the ordinary education in letters of children, but it should precede it. It will not be denied that a child, before it begins to write its alphabet and to gain worldly knowledge, should know what the soul is, what truth is, what love is, what powers are latent in the soul. It should be an essential of real education that a child should learn that, in the struggle of life, it can easily conquer hate by love, untruth by truth, violence by self-suffering. It was because I felt the forces of this truth, that, during the latter part of the struggle, I endeavoured, as much as I could, to train the children at Tolstoy Farm and then at Phœnix along these lines, and one of the reasons for my departure to India is still further to realise, as I already do in part, my own imperfection as a Passive Resister, and then to try to perfect myself, for I believe that it is in India that the nearest approach to perfection is most possible.

SPEECH AT THE JOHANNESBURG BANQUET

[*A Banquet was given at Johannesburg to Mr. and Mrs. Gandhi on the eve of their departure for India, by a large number of Europeans and Indians when Mr. Gandhi said*] :—

Mr. Gandhi said that they or circumstances had placed him that evening in a most embarrassing position. Hitherto those who had known him in Johannesburg had known him in the capacity of one of many hosts at gatherings of that kind, but that evening they had placed him in the unfortunate position of being a guest, and he did not know how he would be able to discharge that duty. For the other he thought long experience had fitted him, if he might say so with due humility, most admirably; but the present position was entirely new to him and Mrs. Gandhi, and he was exceedingly diffident as to how he was going to discharge the new duty that had been imposed upon him. So much had been said about Mrs. Gandhi and himself, their so-called devotion, their so-called self-sacrifice, and many other things. There was one injunction of his religion, and he thought it was true of all religions, and that was that when one's praises were sung one should fly from those praises, and, if one could not do that, one should stop one's ears, and if one could not do either of these things one should dedicate, everything that was said in connection with one to the Almighty, the Divine Essence, which pervaded everyone and everything in the Universe, and he hoped that Mrs. Gandhi and he would have the strength to dedicate all that had been said that evening to that Divine Essence.

Of all the precious gifts that had been given to them those four boys were the most precious, and probably Mr. Chamney could tell them something of the law of adoption in India and what Mr. and Mrs. Naidoo, both of them old gaol-birds, had done. They had gone through the ceremony of adoption, and they had surrendered their right to their four children and given them (Mr. and Mrs. Gandhi) the charge. He did not know that they were worthy to take charge of those children. He could only assure them that they would try to do their best. The four boys had been his pupils when he had been conducting a school for Passive Resisters at Tolstoy Farm and later on at Phœnix. Then when Mrs. Naidoo had sought imprisonment, the boys had been taken over to

Johannesburg, and he thought that he had lost those four pearls, but the pearls had returned to him. He only hoped that Mrs. Gandhi and he would be able to take charge of the precious gift.

Johannesburg was not a new place to him. He saw many friendly faces there, many who had worked with him in many struggles in Johannesburg. He had gone through much in life. A great deal of depression and sorrow had been his lot, but he had also learnt during all those years to love Johannesburg even though it was a Mining Camp. It was in Johannesburg that he had found his most precious friends. It was in Johannesburg that the foundation for the great struggle of Passive Resistance was laid in the September of 1906. It was in Johannesburg that he had found a friend, a guide, and a biographer in the late Mr. Doke. It was in Johannesburg that he had found in Mrs. Doke a loving sister, who had nursed him back to life, when he had been assaulted by a countryman who had misunderstood his mission and who misunderstood what he had done. It was in Johannesburg that he had found a Kallenbach, a Polak, a Miss Schlesin, and many another who had always helped him, and always cheered him and his countrymen. Johannesburg, therefore had the holiest associations of all the holy associations that Mrs. Gandhi and he would carry back to India, and, as he had already said on many another platform, South Africa, next to India, would be the holiest land to him and to Mrs. Gandhi and to his children, for, in spite of all the bitternesses, it had given them those life-long companions. It was in Johannesburg again that the European Committee had been formed, when Indians were going through the darkest stage in their history, presided over then, as it still was, by Mr. Hosken. It was last, but not least, Johannesburg that had given Valiamma, that young girl, whose picture rose before him even as he spoke, who had died in the cause of truth. Simple-minded in faith—she had not the knowledge that he had, she did not know what Passive Resistance was, she did not know what it was the community would gain, but she was simply taken up with unbounded enthusiasm for her people—went to gaol, came out of it a wreck, and within a few days died. It was Johannesburg again that produced a Nagappan and Naryansamy, two lovely youths hardly out of their teens, who also died. But both Mrs. Gandhi and he stood living before them. He and Mrs. Gandhi had worked in the lime light; those others had worked behind the scenes, not knowing where they were going, except this, that what they were doing was right and proper, and, if any praise was due anywhere at all, it was due to those three who died. They had had the name of Harbatsingh given to them. He (the speaker) had had the privilege of serving imprisonment with him. Harbatsingh was 75 years old. He was an ex-indentured Indian, and when he (the speaker) asked him why he had come there, that he had gone there to seek his grave, the brave man replied, "What does it matter? I know what you are fighting for. You have not to pay the £3 tax, but my fellow ex-indentured Indians have to pay that tax, and what more glorious death could I meet?" He had met that death in the gaol at Durban. No wonder if Passive Resistance had fired and quickened the conscience of South Africa! And, therefore, whenever he had spoken, he had said that, if the Indian community had gained anything through this settlement it was certainly due to Passive Resistance; but it was certainly not due to Passive Resistance alone. He thought that the cablegram that had been read that evening showed that they had to thank that noble Viceroy, Lord Hardinge, for his great effort. He thought, too, that they had to thank the Imperial Government, who, during the past few years, in season and out of season, had been sending despatches after despatches to General Botha, and asking him to consider their standpoint—the Imperial standpoint. They had to thank also the Union Government for the spirit of justice they had adopted that time. They had, too, to thank the noble members of both Houses of the Legislature who had made those historic speeches and brought about the settlement; and, lastly, they had to thank the Opposition also for their co-operation with the Government in bringing about the passage of the Bill, in spite of the jarring note produced by the Natal Members. When one considered all those things, the service that he and Mrs. Gandhi might have rendered could be only very little. They were but two out of many instruments that had gone to make this settlement. And what was that settlement? In his humble opinion, the value of the settlement, if they were to examine it, would consist not in the intrinsic things they had received, but in the sufferings and the sorrows long drawn out that were necessary in order to achieve those things. If an outsider were to come there and find that there was a banquet given to two humble individuals for the humble part they played in a settlement which freed indentured Indians from a tax which they should never have been called upon to pay, and if he were told also that some redress were given in connection with their marriages, and that their wives who were lawfully married to them according to their own religions had not hitherto been recognised as their wives, but by this settlement those wives were recognised as valid wives according to the law of South Africa, that outsider would laugh, and consider that those Indians, or those Europeans who had joined them in having a banquet, and giving all those praises and so on, must be a parcel of fools. What was there to gloat over in having an intolerable burden removed which might have been removed years ago? What was there in a lawful wife's being recognised in a place like South Africa? But, proceeded Mr. Gandhi, he concurred with Mr. Duncan in an article he wrote some years ago, when he truly analysed the struggle, and said that behind that struggle for concrete rights lay the great spirit which asked for an abstract principle, and the fight which was undertaken in 1906, although it was a fight against a particular law, was a fight undertaken in order to combat the spirit that was seen about to overshadow the whole of South Africa and to undermine the glorious British Constitution, of which the Chairman had spoken so loftily that evening, and about which he (the speaker) shared his views. It was his knowledge, right or wrong, of the British Constitution which bound him to the Empire. Tear that Constitution to shreds and his loyalty also would be torn to shreds. Keep that Constitution intact, and they held him bound a slave to that Constitution. He had felt that the choice lay for himself and his fellow-countrymen between two courses, when this spirit was brooding over South Africa, either to sunder themselves from the British Constitution, or to fight in order that the ideals of that Constitution might be preserved—but only the ideals. Lord Ampthill had said, in a preface to Mr.

Doke's book, that the theory of the British Constitution must be preserved at any cost if the British Empire was to be saved from the mistakes that all the previous Empires had made. Practice might bend to the temporary aberration through which local circumstances might compel them to pass, it might bend before unreasoning or unreasonable prejudice, but theory once recognised could never be departed from, and this principle must be maintained at any cost. And it was that spirit which had been acknowledged now by the Union Government, and acknowledged how nobly and loftily. The words that General Smuts so often emphasised still rang in his ears. He had said, "Gandhi, this time we want no misunderstanding, we want no mental or other reservations, let all the cards be on the table, and I want you to tell me wherever you think that a particular passage or word does not read in accordance with your own reading," and it was so. That was the spirit in which he approached the negotiations. When he remembered General Smuts of a few years ago, when he told Lord Crewe that South Africa would not depart from its policy of racial distinction, that it was bound to retain that distinction, and that, therefore, the sting that lay in this Immigration Law would not be removed, many a friend, including Lord Ampthill, asked whether they could not for the time being suspend their activity. He had said "No." If they did that it would undermine his loyalty, and even though he might be the only person he would still fight on. Lord Ampthill had congratulated him, and that great nobleman had never deserted the cause even when it was at its lowest ebb, and they saw the result that day. They had not by any means to congratulate themselves on a victory gained. There was no question of a victory gained, but the question of the establishment of the principle that, so far as the Union of South Africa at least was concerned, its legislation would never contain the racial taint, would never contain the colour disability. The practice would certainly be different. There was the Immigration Law—it recognised no racial distinctions, but in practice they had arranged, they had given a promise, that there should be no undue influx from India as to immigration. That was a concession to present prejudice. Whether it was right or wrong was not for him to discuss then. But it was the establishment of that principle which had made the struggle so important in the British Empire, and the establishment of that principle which had made those sufferings perfectly justifiable and perfectly honourable, and he thought that, when they considered the struggle from that standpoint, it was a perfectly dignified thing for any gathering to congratulate itself upon such a vindication of the principles of the British Constitution. One word of caution he wished to utter regarding the settlement. The settlement was honourable to both parties. He did not think there was any room left for misunderstanding, but whilst it was final in the sense that it closed the great struggle, it was not final in the sense that it gave to Indians all that they were entitled to. There was still the Gold Law which had many a sting in it. There was still the Licensing Laws throughout the Union, which also contained many a sting. There was still a matter which the Colonial-born Indians especially could not understand or appreciate, namely, the water-tight compartments in which they had to live; whilst there was absolutely free inter-communication and inter-migration between the Provinces for Europeans, Indians had to be cooped up in their respective Provinces. Then there was undue restraint on their trading activity. There was the prohibition as to holding landed property in the Transvaal, which was degrading, and all these things took Indians into all kinds of undesirable channels. These restrictions would have to be removed. But for that, he thought, sufficient patience would have to be exercised. Time was now at their disposal, and how wonderfully the tone had been changed! And here he had been told in Capetown, and he believed it implicitly, the spirit of Mr. Andrews had pervaded all those statesmen and leading men whom he saw. He came and went away after a brief period, but he certainly fired those whom he saw with a sense of their duty to the Empire of which they were members. But, in any case, to whatever circumstances that healthy tone was due, it had not escaped him. He had seen it amongst European friends whom he met at Capetown; he had seen it more fully in Durban, and this time it had been his privilege to meet many Europeans who were perfect strangers even on board the train, who had come smilingly forward to congratulate him on what they had called a great victory. Everywhere he had noticed that healthy tone. He asked European friends to continue that activity, either through the European Committee or through other channels, and to give his fellow-countrymen their help and extend that fellow-feeling to them also, so that they might be able to work out their own salvation.

To his countrymen he would say that they should wait and nurse the settlement, which he considered was all that they could possibly and reasonably have expected, and that they would now live to see, with the co-operation of their European friends, that what was promised was fulfilled, that the administration of the existing laws was just, and that vested rights were respected in the administration; that after they had nursed these things, if they cultivated European public opinion, making it possible for the Government of the day to grant a restoration of the other rights of which they had been deprived, he did not think that there need be any fear about the future. He thought that, with mutual co-operation, with mutual goodwill, with due response on the part of either party, the Indian community need never be a source of weakness to that Government or to any Government. On the contrary, he had full faith in his countrymen that, if they were well treated, they would always rise to the occasion and help the Government of the day. If they had insisted on their rights on many an occasion, he hoped that the European friends who were there would remember that they had also discharged the responsibilities which had faced them.

And now it was time for him to close his remarks and say a few words of farewell only. He did not know how he could express those words. The best years of his life had been passed in South Africa. India, as his distinguished countryman, Mr. Gokhale, had reminded him, had become a strange land to him. South Africa he knew, but not India. He did not know what impelled him to go to India, but he did know that the parting from them all, the parting from the European friends who had helped him through thick and thin, was a heavy blow, and one he was least able to bear; yet he knew he had to part from them. He could only say farewell and ask them to give him their blessing, to pray for them that their heads might not be turned by the praise they had received, that they might still know how to do their duty to the best of their ability, that they might still learn that first, second, and last should be the approbation of their own conscience, and that then whatever might be due to them would follow in its own time.

INDIANS AND THEIR EMPLOYERS

SPEECH AT VERULAM

[*One of the most important gatherings held just before Mr. Gandhi left South Africa was the great meeting of indentured Indians and employers at Verulam. In his address, Mr. Gandhi took pains to make the position under the Relief Act absolutely clear to the Indian labourers, and addressed a few earnest words at the close to the European Employers of the neighbourhood*] :--

He asked his countrymen to understand that it was wrong for them to consider that the relief that had been obtained had been obtained because he had gone to gaol, or his wife, or those who were immediately near and dear to him. It was because *they* had had the good sense and courage to give up their own lives and to sacrifice themselves, and in these circumstances he had also to tell them that many causes led to that relief, and one of these was certainly also the most valuable and unstinted assistance rendered by Mr. Marshall Campbell of Mount Edgecombe. He thought that their thanks and his thanks were due to him for the magnificent work that he did in the Senate whilst the Bill was passing through it. They would now not have to pay the £3 Tax, and the arrears would also be remitted. That did not mean that they were free from their present indentures. They were bound to go through their present indentures faithfully and honestly, but, when those indentures terminated, they were just as free as any other free Indian, and they were entitled, if they would go to the Protector's office, to the same discharge certificate as was granted to those who came before 1895, under Law 25 of 1891. They were not bound to re-indenture nor to return to India. The discharge certificates would be issued to them free of charge. If they wanted. after having gone to India, to return, they could only do so after they had lived for full three years in the Province as free men after serving their indentures. If any of them wished to have assistance for going to India, they could obtain it from the Government if they did not wish to return from India. If, therefore, they wanted to return from India, they would fight shy of that assistance which was given to them by the Government, but would find their own money or borrow it from friends. If they re-indentured, they could come under the same law, namely, Law 25 of 1891. His own advice to them was not to re-indenture, but by all means to serve their present masters under the common law of the country. If ever occasion arose, which he hoped would never happen, they now knew what it was possible for them to do. But he wanted to remind them of this one thing, that Victoria Country, as also the other Districts of Natal, had not been so free from violence on their own part as the Newcastle District had been. He did not care that provocation had been offered to them or how much they had retaliated with their sticks or with stones, or had burned the sugar cane—that was not passive Resistance, and, if he had been in their midst, he would have repudiated them entirely and allowed his own head to be broken rather than permit them to use a single stick against their opponents. And he wanted them to believe him when he told them that Passive Resistance pure and simple was an infinitely finer weapon than all the sticks and gunpowder put together. They might strike work, but they might compel nobody else to strike work, and, if, as a result of their strike, they were sentenced to be imprisoned, whipped, or to both, they must suffer even unto death—that was Passive Resistance, nothing else. Nothing else, and nothing less than that, would satisfy the requirements of Passive Resistance. If, therefore, he was indentured to Mr. Marshall Campbell, or Mr. Sanders, or any friends about there, and if he found that he was being persecuted or not receiving justice, in their case he would not even go to the Protector, he would sit tight and say, "My master, I want justice or I won't work. Give me food if you want to, water if you want to; otherwise, I sit here hungry and thirsty," and he assured them that the hardest, stoniest heart would be melted. Therefore, let that sink deeply into themselves, that whenever they were afraid of any injury being done to them all, that was the sovereign remedy and that alone was the most effective remedy. If they wanted advice and guidance, and many of them had complained that he was going away, and that his advice would not be at their disposal, all he could suggest to them was that, although he was going away,

MR. A. H. WEST,
joint manager Phoenix Settlement and
" Indian Opinion,"

MR. MAGANLAL K. GHANDI,
Joint Manager Phoenix Settlement and
" Indian Opinion."

Phœnix was not leaving, and, therefore, if they had any difficulty for which they did not wish to pay Mr. Langston or other lawyers, they should go to Phœnix and ask Mr. West or Mr. Chhaganlal Gandhi what was to be done in a particular case. If Mr. West or Mr. Chhaganlal could help them, they would do so free of charge. and if they could not they would send them to Mr. Langston or his other brothers in the law, and he had no doubt that, if they went to Mr. Langston with a certificate from Mr. West that they were too poor, he would render them assistance free of charge. But, if they were called upon to sign any document whatsoever, his advice to them was not to sign it unless they went to Phœnix and got advice. If Phœnix ever failed them and wanted a farthing from them, then they should shun Phœnix.

The scene before him that morning would not easily fade from his memory, even though the distance between him and them might be great. He prayed that God might help them in all the troubles that might be in store for them, and that their conduct might be such that God might find it possible to help them. And to the European friends living in this country he wished to tender his thanks, and he wished also to ask them to forgive him if they had ever considered that during that awful time he was instrumental in bringing about any retaliation at all on the part of his countrymen. He wished to give them this assurance that he had no part or parcel in it, and that, so far as he knew, not a single leading Indian had asked the men to retaliate. There were times in a man's life when he lost his senses, his self-control, and under a sense of irritation, fancied or real, began to retaliate when the brute nature in him rose, and he only went by the law of "might is right," or the law of retaliation—a tooth for a tooth. If his countrymen had done so, whether under a real sense of wrong or fancied, let them forgive him and let them keep a kind corner in their hearts; and, if there were any employers of indentured labour there present who would take that humble request to them, he did ask them not to think always selfishly, though he knew it was most difficult to eradicate self, and let them consider these indentured Indians not merely as cattle which they had to deal with, but as human beings with the same fine feelings, the same fine sentiments as themselves. Let them credit them to the fullest extent with their weaknesses, as also at least with the possibility of all the virtues. Would they not then treat their Indian employees even as brothers ? It was not enough that they were well treated as they well treated their cattle. It was not enough that they looked upon them with a kindly eye merely ; but it was necessary that employers should have a much broader view of their own position, that they should think of their employees as fellow human beings and not as Asiatics who had nothing in common with them who were Europeans, and they would also respond to every attention that might be given to them. Then they would have an intelligent interest not merely in the material or physical well-being of their men, but in their moral well-being. They would look after their morality, after their children, after their education, after their sanitation, and, if they were herding together in such a manner that they could not but indulge in hideous immorality, that they would themselves recoil with horror from the very imagination that the men who were for the time being under their control should indulge in these things because they had been placed in these surroundings. Let them not consider that because these men were drawn from the lowest strata of society that they were beyond reclamation. No, they would respond to every moral pressure that might be brought to bear upon them, and they will certainly realise the moral height that it is possible for every human being, no matter who he is, no matter what tinge of colour his skin possesses.

Mr. & Mrs. GANDHI.

REPLY TO MADRAS PUBLIC RECEPTION

[*The following is the speech delivered by Mr. M. K. Gandhi on the occasion of his visit to Madras in* 1915. *Sir S. Subramania Aiyar presided on the occasion*] :—

MR. CHAIRMAN AND FRIENDS,—On behalf of my wife and myself I am deeply grateful for the honour that you here, and Madras, and, may I say, this presidency, have done to us and the affection that has been lavished upon us in this great and enlightened, not benighted, Presidency. If there is anything that we have deserved, as has been stated in this beautiful address, I can only say I lay it at the feet of my Master under whose inspiration I have been working all this time under exile in South Africa. In so far as the sentiments expressed in this address are merely prophetic, sir, I accept them as a blessing and as a prayer from you and from this great meeting, that both my wife and I myself may possess the power, the inclination, and the life to dedicate whatever may be developed in us by this sacred land of ours to the service of the Motherland. It is no wonder that we have come to Madras. As my friend, Mr. Natesan, will perhaps tell you, we have been long overdue, and we seem to have neglected Madras. But we have done nothing of the kind. We knew that we had a corner in your hearts and we knew that you will not misjudge us if we did not hasten to Madras before going to other Presidencies and other towns. It was in 1896 that I found in Mr. Gokhale my Rajya Guru, and it was here that I found that deep abiding sense of religion which has carried me through all trials. I appeared in 1896 before you as a stranger pleading a forlorn cause, and then discovered that Madras, this Presidency, had that instinctive power to distinguish between a right cause and a wrong cause which marks the religious, and it was here that you appreciated in its fullest measure the gravity of the situation that I was then endeavouring to place before my countrymen throughout India. (Hear, hear). And the impressions that I took with me to South Africa in 1896 have been more than amply verified throughout my experience in South Africa. The drafters of this beautiful address have, I venture to say, exaggerated out of all proportion the importance of the little work that I was able to do in South Africa. (Cries of No, No). As I have said on so many platforms, India is still suffering under the hypnotic influence produced upon it by that great saintly politician, Mr. Gokhale. He assured in my favour a certificate which you have taken at its surface value and it is that certificate which has placed me in a most embarassing position, embarassing because I do not know that I shall be able to answer the expectations that have been raised about myself and about my wife in the work that lies before us in the future on behalf of this country.

But, Sir, if one-tenth of the language that has been used in this address is deserved by us, what language do you propose to use for those who have lost their lives, and therefore finished their work, on behalf of your suffering countrymen in South Africa? What language do you propose to use for Nagappan and Narayanaswami, lads of seventeen or eighteen years, who braved in simple faith all the trials, all the sufferings, and all the indignities for the sake of the honour of the

Motherland? (Applause) What language do you propose to use with reference to Valliamma, that sweet girl of seventeen years, who was discharged from Maritzburg prison, skin and bone, suffering from fever to which she succumbed after about a month's time? (Cries of Shame) It was the Madrasis, who, of all Indians, were singled out by the great Divinity that rules over us for this great work. Do you know that in the great city of Johannesburg, the Madrasis look on a Madrasi dishonoured if he has not passed through the gaols once or twice during this terrible crisis that your countrymen in South Africa went through during these eight long years? You have said that I inspired those great men and women, but I cannot accept that proposition. It was they, the simple-minded folk, who worked away in faith, never expecting slightest reward, who inspired me, who kept me on the proper level, and who combined me by their great sacrifice by their great faith, by their great trust in the great God to do the work that I was able to do. It is my misfortune that I and my wife have been obliged to work in the lime light and you have magnified out of proportion this little

HARBATSINGH,
A Hindustani Stalwart who died in
Durban gaol.

MR. BUDREE AHIR,
A staunch Hindustani Passive Resister.

work we have been able to do. Believe me, my dear friends, that if you consider whether in India or in South Africa it is possible for us, poor mortals, the same individuals, the same stuff of which you are made, if you consider that it is possible for us to do anything whatsoever with your assistance and without your doing the same thing that we would be prepared to do, you are lost, and we are also lost and our services will be in vain. I do not for one moment believe that the inspiration was given by us.

Inspiration was given by them to us, and we were able to be interpreters between the powers who called themselves the Governors and those men for whom redress was so necessary. We were simply links between the two parties and nothing more. It was my duty having received the education that was given, to me by my parents, to interpret what was going on in our midst to those simple folk, and they rose to the occasion. They realised the importance of birth in India, they realised the might of religious force, and it was they who inspired us. Then let these who have finished their work, and who have died for you and me, let them inspire you and us. We are still living, and who knows that the devil will not possess us to-morrow and we shall not forsake the duty ? But these three have gone for ever. An old man of 75 from the United Provinces, Harbat Singh, he has also joined the majority and died in gaol in South Africa, and he deserved the crown that you would seek to impose upon us. These young men deserve all these adjectives that you have so affectionately, but blindly, lavished upon us. It was not only the Hindus who struggled, but there were Muhammadans, Parsis and Christians, and almost every part of India was represented in the struggle. They realised the common danger, and they realised also what their destiny was as Indians, as it was they, and they alone, who matched the soul-force against the physical forces.

MADRAS LAW DINNER

[*Speech delivered by Mr. M. K. Gandhi on the occasion of "Madras Law Dinner" held at Madras on 24th April,* 1915, *under the presidency of the Advocate-General*] :—

MY LORD CHIEF JUSTICE, MR. CHAIRMAN AND GENTLEMEN :—During my three months' tour in India, as also in South Africa, I have been so often questioned how I, a determined opponent of modern civilisation, and avowed patriot, could reconcile myself to loyalty to the British Empire of which India was such a large part, how it was possible for me to find it consistent that India and England could work together for mutual benefit. It gives me the greatest pleasure this evening at this great and important gathering to re-declare my loyalty to the British Empire, and my loyalty is based upon very selfish grounds. As a passive resister I discovered that he has to make good his claim to passive resistance, no matter under what circumstances he finds himself, and I find that the British Empire had certain ideals, with which I have fallen in love, and one of these ideals is that every subject of the British Empire has the freest scope possible for his energies and for whatever he thinks is due to his conscience, I think that this is true of the British Empire, as it is not true of any other Government that we see. I feel, as you have, perhaps, known that I am no lover of any Government, and I have more than once said that the Government is best which governs that least; and I have found that it is possible for me to be governed least under the British Empire hence my loyalty to the British throne.

ADVICE TO STUDENTS

[*Speech delivered at the Y. M. C. A. Madras on 27th April,* 1915, *Hon'ble Mr. V. S. Srinivasa Sastry presiding*] :—

MR. CHAIRMAN AND DEAR FRIENDS:—Madras has well-nigh exhausted the English vocabulary in using adjectives of virtue with reference to my wife and myself and if I may be called upon to give an opinion as to where I have been smoothered with kindness, love and attention, I would have to say it is Madras. (Applause). But as I have said so often, I believed it of Madras. So it is no wonder to me that you are lavishing all these kindnesses with unparalleled generosity, and now the worthy President of the Servants of India Society, under which Society I am now going through a period of probation, has, if I may say so, capped it all. Am I worthy of these things? My answer from the innermost recess of the heart is an emphatic "No." But I have come to India to become worthy of every adjective that you may use, and all my life will certainly be dedicated to prove worthy of them if I am to be a worthy servant. In India's beautiful national song (Bande Mataram) the poet has lavished all the adjectives that he possibly could to describe Mother India. Have we a right to sing that hymn? The poet no doubt gave us a picture for our realisation, the words of which remain simply prophetic, and it is for you, the hope of India, to realise every word that the poet has said in describing this Motherland of ours. To-day I feel that these adjectives are very largely misplaced in his description of the Motherland.

You, the students of Madras as well as the students all over India, are you receiving an education which will make you worthy to realise that ideal, and which will draw the best out of you? Or is it an education which has become a factory for making Government employees, or clerks in commercial offices? Is the goal of the education that you are receiving for mere employment, whether in Government department or in other departments? If that be the goal of your education, if that is the goal that you have set before yourselves, I feel, I fear, that the vision that the poet pictured for himself is far from being realised. As you have heard me say, perhaps, or as you have read, I am, and I have been, a determined opponent of modern civilisation. I want you to turn your eyes to-day upon what is going on in Europe, and if you have come to the conclusion that Europe is to-day groaning under the heels of that modern civilisation, then you and your elders will have to think twice before you emulate that civilisation in our Motherland. But I have been told: " How can we help it, seeing that our Rulers bring that culture to our Motherland ?" Do not make any mistake about it. I do not for one moment believe that it is for our Rulers to bring that culture to you, unless you are prepared to accept it and if it be that the Rulers bring that culture before us, I think that we have forces for ourselves to enable us to reject that culture without having to reject the Rulers themselves. (Applause). I have said on many a platform that the British race is with us. I decline to go into the reasons why that race is with us, but I do not believe that it is possible for India, if it would live up to the traditions of the Sages of whom you have heard from our worthy President, to transmit a message through this great race, a message not of physical might but a message of love. And then it will be your privilege to conquer the conquerors, not by shedding blood but by sheer spiritual predominance. When I consider what is going on in India, I think it is necessary for us to see what our opinion is in connection with the political assasinations and political dacoities. I feel that these are purely a foreign importation, which cannot take root in this land. But you, the student world, have to beware lest, mentally or morally, you give one thought of approval to this kind of terrorism. I as a passive resister will give you another thing very substantial for it. Terrorise yourself; search within; by all means resist tyranny where ever you find it; by all means resist encroachment upon your liberty; but not by shedding the blood of the tyrant. That is not what is taught by our religion. Our religion is based upon *Ahimsa* which in its active form is nothing but love, love not only to your neighbours, not only to your friends, but love even to those who may be your enemies.

One word more in connection with the same thing. I think that if we were to practise truth, to practise *Ahimsa*, we must immediately see that we also practise fearlessness. If our Rulers are doing what in our opinion is wrong, and if we feel it our duty to let them hear our advice, even though it may be considered sedition, I urge you to speak sedition—but at your peril, you must be prepared to suffer the consequences. And when you are ready to suffer the consequences and not hit below the belt, then I think you will have made good your right to have your advice heard even by the Government.

I ally myself to the British Government, because I believe that it is possible for me to claim equal partnership with every subject of the British Empire. I to-day claim that equal partnership. I do not belong to a subject race. I do not call myself a subject race. (Applause). But there is this thing: it is not for the British Governors to give you, it is for you to take the thing. That I want only by discharging my obligations. Max Muller has told us—we need not go to Max Muller to interpret our own religion—but he says our religion consists in four letters D-U-T-Y and not in the five letters R-I-G-H-T. And if you believe that all that we want can go from *a letter*, discharge of our duty then think always of your duty, and fighting along these lines you will have no fear of any man, you will only fear God. That is the message that my Master too, Mr. Gokhale, has given to us, what is that message then ? It is in the constitution of the Servants of India Society, and that it is that message by which I wish to be guided in my life. The message is to spiritualise political life and political institutions of the country. We must immediately set about realising it in practice. Then students cannot be away from politics. Politics is as essential to them as religion. Politics cannot be divorced from religion.

My views may not be acceptable to you I know. All the same, I can only give you what is stirring me to my very depths. On the authority of my experience in South Africa, I claim that your countrymen who had not that modern culture, but who had that strength of the Rishis of old who have inherited the Tapasyacharya performed by the Rishis, without having known a single word of English literature, and without having known anything whatsoever of the present modern culture, were able to rise to their full height. And what has been possible for the uneducated and illiterate countrymen of ours in South Africa is ten times possible for you and for me to-day in this sacred land of ours. May that be your privilege and may that be mine also! (Loud Applause).

BRAHMINS AND PANCHAMAS

[*Mr. and Mrs. Gandhi on their way to Tranquebar arrived at Mayavaram on 2nd May,* 1915, *and they were presented with an address by the citizens of the town. In the course of his reply Mr. Gandhi said*] :—

It was quite by accident that I had the great pleasure, of receiving an address from my ' Panchama brethren,' and there, they said that they were without convenience for drinking water, they were without convenience for living supplies, and they could not buy or hold land. It was difficult for them even to approach courts. Probably, the last is due to their fear, but a fear certainly not due to themselves, and who is then responsible for this state of things ? Do we propose to perpetuate this state of things ? Is it a part of Hinduism ? I do not know. I have now to learn what Hinduism really is. In so far as I have been able to study Hinduism outside India, I have felt that it is no part of real Hinduism to have in its fold a mass of people whom I would call " untouchables," If it was proved to me that this is an essential part of Hinduism, I, for one, would declare myself an open rebel against Hinduism itself. (Hear, hear.)

Are the Brahmins in Mayavaram equiminded towards the Pariah and will they tell me, if they are so equiminded and if so, will they tell me if others will not follow ? Even if they say that they are prepared to do so but others will not follow, I shall have to disbelieve them until I have revised my notions of Hinduism. If the Brahmins themselves consider they are holding high position by penance and posterity, then they have themselves much to learn, then they will be the people who have cursed and ruined the land.

MR. GANDHI AND THE LEADERS

My friend, the Chairman, has asked me the question whether it is true that I am at war with my leaders. I say that I am not at war with my leaders. I seemed to be at war with my leaders because many things I have heard seem to be inconsistent with my notions of self-respect and with self-respect to my Motherland. I feel that they are probably not discharging the sacred trust they have taken upon their shoulders ; but I am not sure I am studying or endeavouring to take wisdom from them, but I failed to take that wisdom. It may be that I am incompetent and unfit to follow them. So, I shall revise my ideas. Still I am in a position to say that I seem to be at war with my leaders. Whatever they do or whatever they say does not somehow or other appeal to me. The major part of what they say does not seem to be appealing to me.

ENGLISH AND THE VERNACULARS

I find here words of welcome in the English language. I find in the Congress programme a Resolution on Swadeshi. If you hold that you are Swadeshi and yet print these in English, then I am not a Swadeshi. To me it seems that it is inconsistent. I have nothing to say against the English language. But I do say that, if you kill the vernaculars and raise the English language on the tomb of the vernaculars (hear, hear), then you are not favouring Swadeshi in the right sense of the term. If you feel that I do not know Tamil, you should pardon me, you should excuse me and teach me and ask me to learn Tamil and by having your welcome in that beautifnl language, if you translate it to me, then I should think you are performing some part of the programme. Then only I should think I am being taught Swadeshi.

SWADESHI ENTERPRISE

I asked when we were passing through Mayavaram whether there have been any handlooms here and whether there were handloom weavers here. I was told that there were 50 handlooms in Mayavaram. What were they engaged in? They were simply engaged chiefly in preparing "Sarees" for our women. Then is Swadeshi to be confined only to the women? Is it to be only in their keeping? I do not find that our friends, the male population also have their stuff prepared for them in these by these weavers and through their handlooms, (a voice there are a thousand handlooms here). There are, I understand, one thousand handlooms so much the worse for the leaders! (Loud applause.) If these one thousand handlooms are kept chiefly in attending to the wants of our women, double this supply of our handlooms and you will have all your wants supplied by your own weavers and there will be no poverty in the land. I ask you and ask our friend the President how far he is indebted to foreign goods for his outfit and if he can tell me that he has tried his utmost and still has failed to outfit himself or rather to fit himself out with Swadeshi clothing and therefore he has got this stuff, I shall sit at his feet and learn a lesson. What I have been able to learn to-day is that it is entirely possible for me, not with any extra cost to fit myself with Swadeshi clothing. How am to I learn through those who move or who are supposed to be movers in the Congress, the secret of the Resolution. I sit at the feet of my leaders, I sit at the feet of Mayavaram people and let them reveal the mystery, give me the secret of the meaning, teach me how I should behave myself and tell me whether it is a part of the National movement that I should drive off those who are without dwellings, who cry for water and that I should reject the advances of those who cry for food. These are the questions which I ask my friends here. Since I am saying something against you, I doubt whether I shall still enjoy or retain the affection of the student population and whether I shall still retain the blessing of my leaders. I ask you to have a large heart and give me a little corner in it. I shall try to steal into that corner. If you would, be kind enough to teach me the wisdom, I shall learn the wisdom in all humility and in all earnestness. I am praying for it, and I am asking for it. If you cannot teach me, I again declare myself at war with my leaders. (Loud cheers).

REPLY TO NELLORE CONFERENCE

[*Replying to a complimentary Resolution moved at the Madras Provincial Conference at Nellore, Mr. Gandhi said*]:—

It was an accident that this Resolution followed on two Resolutions, one with reference to his revered master and the other with reference to the noble Viceroy to whom a fitting tribute had been paid by the President. He was there free to acknowledge the indebtedness of his countrymen in South Africa to the noble Viceroy. If his wife and he were worthy of anything that had been said on this platform and on many a platform, he had repeated, and he was there again to repeat, that they owed all to the inspiration they derived from Indian sources, for it was Mr. Gokhale, his love, and his message, that had been his guiding star, and would still remain his guiding star. He would appeal to them not to spoil him and his wife by taking away from the services they had to render by over-praising them. He would make this simple, but humble, appeal. Let what he and his wife had done in South Africa be buried there. Their countrymen in South Africa would know what had been done. It was impossible for any one, much less for them, to trade on any reputation made in South Africa. He feared that by overpraising them, they might raise enormous expectations about him and his wife that they might in the end, he would not say it was hardly likely, meet with disappointment.

REPLY TO BANGALORE PUBLIC

[*An address was presented to Mr. and Mrs. Gandhi by the citizens of Bangalore, on 8th May,* 1915, *to which Mr. Gandhi replied as follows*] :—

MR. CHAIRMAN AND MY FRIENDS,—I think it is simply impertinent to tell you that I thank you most sincerely on behalf of my wife and on my own behalf for the signal honour you have shown me. Words fail me, and one thought oppresses me all the more. Am I, are we, worthy of the honour ? Are we worthy of the oriental generosity of this love ? The Chairman has furnished this ground for the love, and quoted Mr. Gokhale. Let me not bask in that reputation. See me please in the nakedness of my working, and in my limitations, you will then know me. I have to tread on most delicate grounds, and my path is destined to be through jungles and temples. The glamour produced by the saintly politician has vanished, and let us be judged eye to eye. So many have assembled here to do honour. This morning, you did greater honour. Greater honour was shown by the Reception Committee in arranging for the conversation, in order to open my heart to you and to understand the inner-most thoughts in you by quiet conversation between my countrymen and myself.

I did not want to be dragged. There is a meaning. Let us not be dragged. Let them work silently. We should not encourage the thought that workers will be honoured similarly. Let public men feel that they will be stoned, that they will be neglected, and let them feel they still love the country. A charge has been brought against us that we are too demonstrative and lack business-like methods. We plead guilty to the charge. Are we to copy modern activities, or are we to copy the ancient civilisation, which has survived so many shocks? You and I have to act on the political platform from the spiritual side, and if this is done, we shall then conquer the conquerors. The day will dawn then, when we can consider an Englishman as a fellow-citizen (Cheers). That day will shortly come, but it may be difficult to conceive. I have had signal opportunities of associating myself with Englishmen of character, devotion, nobility and influence. I can assure you that the present wave of activity is passing away, and a new civilisation is coming shortly, which will be a nobler one.

India is a great dependency and Mysore is a great Native State. It must be possible for you to transmit this message to British Governors and to British statesmen ; the message is: establish a *Rama Rajya* in Mysore and have your minister a Vashista, who will command obedience. My fellow countrymen, then you can dictate terms to the conquerors. (Prolonged Cheers).

MR. GANDHI ON MR. GOKHALE

[*In unveiling the portrait of Mr. Gokhale in Bangalore, Mr. Gandhi spoke as follows*] :—

MY DEAR COUNTRYMEN,—Before I perform this ceremony to which you have called me, I wish to say this to you that you have given me a great opportunity or rather a privilege on this great occasion. I saw in the recitation —the beautiful recitation that was given to me,—that God is with them whose garment was dusty and tattered. My thoughts immediately went to the end of my garment; I examined and found that it is not dusty and it is not tattered; it is fairly spotless and clean. God is not in me. There are other conditions attached; but in these conditions too I may fail; and you, my dear countrymen, may also fail; and if we do tend this well, we should not dishonour the memory of one whose portrait you have asked me to unveil this morning. I have declared myself his disciple in the political field and I have him as my *Rajya Guru*; and this I claim on behalf of the Indian people. It was in 1896 that I made this declaration, and I do not regret having made the choice.

Mr. Gokhale taught me that the dream of every Indian who claims to love his country, should be to act in the political field, should be not to glorify in language, but to spiritualise the political life of the country, and the political institutions of the country. He inspired my life and is still inspiring: and in that I wish to purify myself and spiritualise myself. I have dedicated myself to that ideal. I may fail, and to what extent I may fail, I call myself to that extent an unworthy disciple of my master.

SPIRITUALISING THE POLITICAL LIFE

What is the meaning of spiritualising the political life of the country? What is the meaning of spiritualising myself? That question has come before me often and often and to you it may seem one thing, to me it may seem another thing; it may mean different things to the different members of the Servants of India Society itself. It shows much difficulty and it shows the difficulties of all those who want to love their country, who want to serve their country and who want to honour their country. I think the political life must be an echo of private life and that there cannot be any divorce between the two. * *

I was by the side of that saintly politician to the end of his life and I found no ego in him. I ask you members of the Social Service League, if there is no ego in you. If he wanted to shine, he wanted to shine in the political field of his country, he did so not in order that he might gain public applause, but in order that his country may gain. He developed every particular faculty in him, not in order to win the praise of the world for himself but in order that his country may gain. He did not seek public applause, but they were showered upon him, they were thrust upon him; he wanted that his country may gain and that was his great inspiration.

There are many things for which India is blamed, very rightly, and if you should add one more to our failures the blame will descend not only on you but also on me for having participated in to-day's functions. But I have great faith in my countrymen.

You ask me to unveil this portrait to-day,

and I will do so in all sincerity and sincerity should bo the end of your life. (Loud and continued applause).

A TALK WITH MR. GANDHI

[*Questioned as to India's poverty, Mr. Gandhi said India was becoming poorer and poorer, on account of the disappearance of the handloom industries owing to violent competition and export of raw materials*] :—

"We have lost" he said, "much of our self-respect, on account of being too much Europeanised. We think and speak in English. Thereby, we impoverish our vernaculars, and estrange the feelings of the masses. A knowledge of English is not very essential to the service of our Motherland." Turning to caste, he said "caste is the great power and secret of Hinduism."

Asked where he would stay, Mr. Gandhi replied: "Great pressure is brought down on me to settle in Bengal; but I have a great capital in the store of my knowledge in Guzerat and I get letters from there."

"Vernacular literature is important. I want to have a library of all books. I invite friends for financial aid to form libraries and locate them."

" Modern civilisation is a curse in Europe as also in India. War is the direct result of modern civilisation, everyone of the Powers was making preparations for war."

" Passive Resistance is a great moral force, meant for the weak, also for the strong. Soul-force depends on itself. Ideals must work in practice, otherwise they are not potential. Modern civilisation is a brute force."

It is one thing to know the ideal and another thing to practise it. That will ensure greater discipline, which means a greater service and greater service means greater gain to Government. Passive resistance is a highly aggressive thing. The attribute of soul is restlessness; there is room for every phase of thought.

" Money land and women are the sources of evil and evil has to be counteracted. I need not possess land, nor a woman, nor money to satisfy my luxuries. I do not want to be unhinged because others are unhinged. If ideals are practised, there will be less room *for* mischievous activities. Public life has to be moulded."

" Every current has to change its course.

There are one and a half million sadhus and if every sadhu did his duty, India could achieve much. Jagat Guru Sankaracharya does not deserve that apellation because he has no more force in him."

Malicious material activity is no good. It finds out means to multiply one's luxuries. Intense gross modern activity should not be imposed on Indian institutions, which have to be remodelled on ideals taken from Hinduism. Virtue as understood in India is not understood in foreign lands. Dasaratha is considered a fool in foreign lands, for his having kept his promise to his wife. India says a promise is a promise. That is a good ideal. Material activity is mischievous. "Truth shall conquer in the end."

"Emigration does no good to the country from which people emigrate. Emigrants do not return better moral men. The whole thing is against Hinduism. Temples do not flourish. There are no opportunities for ceremonial functions. Priests do not come, and at times, they are merely men of straw. Immigrants play much mischief and corrupt society. It is not enterprise. They may earn more money easily in those parts which means, they do not want to toil and remain straight in the methods of earning. Immigrants are not happier and have more material wants."

Questioned about the Theosophical Society Mr. Gandhi said: "There is a good deal of good in the Theosophical Society, irrespective of individuals. It has stimulated ideas and thoughts.

BENARES INCIDENT

[There appeared in the 'New India' a charge against Mr. Gandhi as having spoken something to be taken an exception to by the public while addressing a large audience at the "Hindu University Pavilion," Benares to which Mr. Gandhi replied as under] :—

Mrs. Besant's reference in *New India* and certain other references to the Benares incident perhaps render it necessary for me to return to the subject, however disinclined I may be to do so. Mrs. Besant denies my statement with reference to her whispering to the Princes. I can only say that if I can trust my eyes and my ears I must adhere to the statement I have made. She occupied a seat on the left of the semi-circle on either side of the Maharaja of Dharbanga, who occupied the Chair, and there was at least one Prince, perhaps, there were two who were sitting on her side. Whilst I was speaking Mrs. Besant was almost behind me. When the Maharajas rose Mrs. Besant also had risen. I had ceased speaking before the Rajas actually left the platform. She was discussing the incident with a group round her on the platform. I gently suggested to her that she might have refrained from interrupting, but that if she disapproved of the speech after it was finished she could have then dissociated herself from my sentiments. But she, with some degree of warmth, said: "How could we sit still when you were compromising every one of us on the platform? You ought not to have made the remarks you did." This answer of Mrs. Besant's does not quite tally with her solicitude for me which alone, according to her version of the incident, prompted her to interrupt the speech. I suggest that if she merely meant to protect me she could have passed a note round or whispered into my ears her advice. And, again, if it was for my protection why was it necessary for her to rise with Princes and to leave the hall as I hold she did along with them?

So far as my remarks are concerned I am yet unable to know what it was in my speech that seems to her to be open to such exception as to warrant her interruption. After referring to the Viceregal visit and the necessary precautions that were taken for the Viceroy's safety I showed that an assasins death was anything but honourable death and said that anarchism was opposed to our Shastras and had no room in India. I said then where there was an honourable death it would go down to history as men who died for their conviction. But when a bomb thrower died, secretly plotting all sorts of things, what could he gain? I then went on to state and deal the fallacy that, had not bomb throwers thrown bombs we should never have gained what we did with reference to the Partition movement. It was at about this stage that Mrs. (Besant appealed to the chair to stop me. Personally, I will desire a publication of the whole of my speech whose trend was a sufficient warrant for showing that I could not possibly incite the students to deeds of violence. Indeed it was conceived in order to carry on a rigorous self-examination.

I began by saying that it was a humiliation for the audience and myself that I should have to speak in English. I said that English having been the medium of instruction it had done a tremendous injury to the country, and as I conceive I showed successfully that, had we received training during the past 50 years in higher thought in our own vernaculars, we would be to-day within reach of our goal. I then referred to the self-government Resolution passed at the Congress and showed that whilst the All-India Congress Committee and the All-India Muslim League would be drawing up their paper about the future constitution their duty was to fit themselves by their own action for self-government. And in order to show how short we feel of our duty I drew attention to the dirty condition of the labyrinth of lanes surrounding the great temple of Kasi Visvanath and the recently erected palatial buildings without any conception as to the straightness or width of the streets. I then took the audience to the gorgeous scene that was enacted on the day of the foundation and suggested that if a stranger not knowing anything about Indian life had visited the scene he would have gone away under the false impression that India was one of the richest countries in the world,—such was the display of jewellery worn by our noblemen. And turning to the Maharajas and the Rajahs I humourously suggested that it was necessary for them to hold those treasurers in trust for the nation before we could realise our ideals, and I cited the action of the Japanese noblemen who considered it a glorious privilege even though there was no necessity for them, to dispossess themselves of the treasures and lands which were handed to them from generation to generation. I then asked the audience to consider the humiliating spectacle of the Viceroy's person having to be protected from ourselves when he was our honoured guest. And I was endeavouring to show that the blame for these precautions was also on ourselves in that they were rendered necessary because of the introduction of organised assassination in India. Thus I was endeavouring to show on the one hand how the students could usefully occupy themselves in assisting to rid the society of its proved defects, on the other, to wean themselves even in thought from methods of violence.

I claim that with twenty years' experience of public life in the course of which I had to address on scores of occasions turbulant audiences. I have some experience of feeling the pulse of my audience. I was following closely how the speech was being taken and I certainly did not notice that the student world was being adversely affected. Indeed some of them came to me the following morning and told me that they perfectly understood my remarks which had gone home. One of them a keen debater even subjected to cross-examination and seemed to feel convinced by a further development of the argument such as I had advanced in the course of my speech. Indeed I have spoken now to thousands of students and others of my countrymen throughout South Africa, England and India ; and by precisely the arguments that I used that evening I claimed to have weaned many from their approval of anarchical methods.

Finally, I observe that Mr. S. S. Setlur of Bombay, who has written on the incident to the Hindu in no friendly mood towards me, and who I think in some respects totally unfairly has endeavoured to tear me to pieces, and who was an eye witness to the proceedings, gives a version different from Mrs. Besant's. He thinks that the general impression was not that I was encouraging the anarchists but that I was playing the role of an apologist for the Civilian bureaucrat. The whole of Mr. Setlur's attack upon me shows that if he is right I was certainly not guilty of any incitement to violence and that the offence consisted in my reference to jewellery, etc.

In order that the fullest justice might be done both to Mrs. Besant and myself I would make the following suggestion. She says that she does not propose to defend herself by quoting the sentence which drove the Princes away and that would be playing into the enemy's hands; according to her previous statement my speech is already in the hands of the detectives so that so far as my safety is concerned her forbearance is not going to be of the slightest use. Would it not therefore be better that she should either publish a verbatim report if she has it or reproduce such sentiments in my speech as in her opinion, necessitated her interruption and the Princes' withdrawal.

I will therefore conclude this statement by repeating what I have said before; that but for Mrs. Besant's interruption I would have concluded my speech within a few minutes and no possible misconception about my views on anarchism would have arisen.

INDENTURED LABOUR

The question of indentured labour is a seasonable subject for more reasons than one. Messrs. Andrews and Pearson have just returned from Fiji after finishing their self-imposed labours for the sake of India which they have learnt to love as they love their motherland. Their report is about to be issued. There Mr. Malaviya has given notice for leave to move a resolution in the Imperial Council which will if adopted, commit the Government to a repeal of the system of indentured labour. Mr. Malaviya's resolution will be, it may be decided, a continuation of the late Mr. Gokhale's work in 1912, when in a speech full of fervour and weighted with facts and figures he moved his resolution demanding repeal of this form of labour. The deceased stateman's resolution was thrown out only by the force of official majority. The moral victory lay with Mr. Gokhale. The deathknell of the system was rung when that resolution was moved. The Government, as it could not then

REV. C. F. ANDREWS, AND
MR. W. W. PEARSON,
Who went to S. Africa during the late crisis
to offer their **services as mediators.**

REV. J. J. DOKE,
Foremost Exponent of Passive Resistance.
Biographer of Mr. Gandhi.

abolish the system, outvoted Mr. Gokhale but did not fail to note that they must hurry forward to do so at an early date. Mr. Malaviya's proposed resolution and the report of Messrs. Andrews and Pearson, which latter, it is known, is to suggest total abolition of the system, will enable Lord Hardinge fittingly to close his most eventful viceroyalty removing this longstanding and acknowledged grievance.

These lines will be merely an attempt to give personal observations and to indulge in a few reflections upon the question. For facts and figures the reader and the public worker must look up Mr. Gokhale's speech referred to above and Messrs. Andrews and Pearson's forthcoming report.

Indentured labour is admittedly a remnant of slavery. The late Sir William Wilson Hunter, when his attention was drawn to it in 1895, was the first to call it a state perilously near to slavery. Most legislation only partly reflects the public opinion of its time. Legislation abolishing slavery was really a bit in advance of public opinion, and that was a big bit. And its effect, like that of all such legislation was largely neutralised by the dissatisfied slave-owners resorting to the dodge of indentured labour. The yoke, if it fell from the Negro's black neck, was transferred to the brown neck of the Indian. In the process of transfer, it had somewhat to be somewhat polished, it had to be lightened in weight and even disguised. Nevertheless in all its essentials it retained its original quality. The hideousness of the system was forcefully demonstrated when the curse descended upon South Africa in the shape of indentured labourers from China for working the gold mines. It was no mere election cry that the late Sir Henry Campbell Bannerman had taken up when he made the British Isles from end to end ring with denunciation of the system. No cost was counted as too great for ridding South Africa of the evil. The great multimillionaires of Johannesburgh spared nothing to be enabled to hold to the indentured Chinaman, They asked for breathing-time. The House of Commons remained unmoved. Mine-owners had to shift for themselves. The interest of humanity overrode all other considerations. The mines were threatened to be closed. The House did not care. The millions promised to Mr. Chamberlain would not be forthcoming. The House laughed. Within six months of passage of the measure for the abolition of Chinese indentured labour, every Chinese labourer had been repatriated bag and baggage. The mines survived the shock. They discovered other methods of life. And now be it said to the credit of the mine-owners as well as of the Conservatives who opposed the measure, that both these classes recognise that the abolition was a great deliverance.

Indian indentured labours is not less demoralising. It has persisted because its bitterness like that of a sugared pill has been cleverly though unconsciously concealed. The one great distinction between the two classes was that the Chinese were brought in without a single woman with them, whereas every hundred Indian labourers must include forty women among them. Had the Chinese remained they would have sapped the very foundations of the society. The Indian labourers confine the evil to themselves. This may be unimportant to non-Indians. But for us, the wonder is that we have allowed the sin to continue so long. The business about the women is the weakest and the irremediable part of the evil. It therefore needs a somewhat closer inspection. These women are not necessarily wives. Men and women are huddled together during the voyage. The marriage is a farce. A mere declaration by man and woman made upon landing before the Protector of immigrants that they are husband and wife constitutes a valid marriage. Naturally enough divorce is common. The rest must be left to the imagination of the reader. This is certain—that the system does not add to the moral well-being of India. And it is suggested that no amount of figures adduced to show that the labourer is far richer at the end of his contract of labour than when he entered upon it can be allowed to be any set-off against the moral degradation it involves.

There is another most powerful consideration to be urged against the continuance of this system. The relations between Englishmen and Indians in India are not of the happiest. The average Englishman considers himself to be superior to the average Indian and the latter is generally content to be so considered. Such a state of things is demoralising to both and a meance to the stability. of the British

Empire. There is no reason why every Englishman should not learn to consider every Indian as his brother and why should not every Indian cease to think that he is born to fear every Englishman. Be that as it may, this unnatural relationship is reflected in an exaggerated form outside India when the artificial state of indentured service under a white employer is set up. Unless, therefore, the relation between the English and ourselves is put on a correct footing in India, and transference of Indian labourers to far off lands whether parts of the Empire or otherwise, even under a free contract must harm both employer and employed. I happen to have the privilege of knowing most humane employers of Indian labourers in Natal. They were their men. But they do not, they cannot give them more than the most favoured treatment that their cattle receive. I use this language in no uncharitable spirit. The humanest of employers cannot escape the limitations of his class. He instinctively feels that the Indian labourer is inferior to him and can never be equal to him. Surely no indentured Indian, no matter how clever and faithfull he may be, has ever inherited his master's state. But I know English servants who have risen to their master's state even as Indian servants have risen to their Indian master's state. It is not the Englishman's fault that the relationship with his Indian employees has not been progressive. It is beyond the scope of these lines to distribute the blame, if there is any, on either side or to examine the causes for the existence of such a state of things. I have been obliged to advert to it to show that apart from all other considerations, the system of indentured labour is demonstrably so degrading to us as a nation that it must be stopped at any cost and that now.

THE NEED OF INDIA

[*Mr. M. K. Gandhi delivered an address to the students at the Y. M. C. A. auditorium, Madras* (1915) *with the Hon. Rev. G. Pittendrigh in the chair, in the course of which he said*] :—

I did not know what subject to choose. A friend has handed me a slip here, asking me whether I would not enlighten the students on the Benares incident. I fear that I shall have to disappoint that friend and those of you who associate yourselves with that view. I do not think you need lay any stress upon that incident. Those are the passing waves which will always come and go. I would rather this morning, if I can possibly do so, pour my soul out to you with reference to something which I treasure so much above everything else. To many students who came to me last year, I said I was about to establish an Ashrama somewhere in India, and it is about that place that I am going to talk to you to-day.

THE NEED OF INDIA

I have felt during the whole of my public life that what we need, what any Nation needs, but we perhaps of all the other Nations of the world need just now, is nothing else and nothing less than character-building. You know that Mr. Gokhale used so often to say that our average was less than the average of so many European Nations. I do not know whether that statement of him, whom with pride I consider to be my political Guru, has really foundation in fact. But I do believe that there is much to be said to justify that statement in so far as the educated India is concerned, not because the educated portion of the community blundered, but because we have been creatures of circumstances. Be that as it may; this is the maxim of life which I have accepted, namely, that no work done by any man, no matter how great he is, will really prosper unless it has a religious backing. By religion, I do not mean the religion which you will get after reading all the scriptures of the world; it is not really a grasp by the brain, but it is the heart-grasp. It is a thing which is not evident to us, but it is a thing which is evolved out of us; it is always within us, with some, consciously so, with the others quite unconsciously, but it is there, and whether we wake up this religious instinct in us through outside assistance or by inward growth, no matter how it is done, it has got to be done if we want to do anything in the right manner and anything that is going to persist. Our scriptures have laid down certain rules as maxims of life, which we have to take for granted, and believing in these maxims implicitly for all these long years and having actually endeavoured to reduce to practice those injunctions of the Shastras, I have deemed it necessary to seek the association of those who think with me in founding this Institution. I shall place before you this morning the rules that have been drawn up and that have to be observed by everyone who seeks to be a member of that Ashrama.

VOW OF TRUTH

There are five rules known as Yamas, and the first is the vow of truth, not truth as we ordinarily understand it, but truth which means that we have to rule our life by the law of truth at any cost, and in order to satisfy the definition I have drawn upon the celebrated illustration of the life of Prahalada, who, for the sake of truth, dared to oppose his own father. In this Ashrama we make it a rule that we must say no when we mean no, regardless of consequences.

VOW OF AHIMSA

The next rule is the vow of Ahimsa, which means non-killing. To me, it has a world of meaning, and takes me into realms much higher than the realms to which I would go if I merely understood Ahimsa to mean non-killing. Ahimsa really means that you may not offend anybody, you may not harbour an uncharitable thought even in connection with one who may consider himself to be your enemy. For one who follows the doctrine of Ahimsa, there is no room for the enemy. Under this rule, there is no room for organised assassination, and there is no room for murders even openly committed, and there is no room for violence even for the sake of your country and even for guarding the honour of precious ones that may be under your charge. This doctrine of Ahimsa tells us that we may guard the honour of those who are under our charge by delivering ourselves into the hands of the men who would commit the sacrilege, and that requires far greater physical and mental courage than delivering blows. You may have some degree of physical power—I do not say courage—and you may use that power, but after it is expended, what happens? The man is wild with wrath and indignation, and you have made him wilder by matching your violence against his, and when he has done you to death, the rest of his violence is delivered on to your charge; but if you do not retaliate but simply stand your ground to receive all the blows and stand between your charge and the opponent, what happens? I give you my promise that the whole violence will be expended on you, and your charge will be left sacred.

VOW OF CELIBACY

Those who want to perform National Service or those who want to have the glimpse of real religious life must lead a celibate life, whether married or unmarried. Marriage brings a woman close together with a man, and they become friends in a special sense, never to be parted either in this life or in the lives that are to come; but I do not think that into that plane of life our lusts should necessarily enter.

CONTROL OF PALATES

Then there is the vow of the control of the palates. A man who wants to control his animal passion easily does so without even noticing that he does so. Without being a slave to his palate, he will master his palate. This is one of the most difficult vows to follow. I am just now coming from having inspected the Victoria Hostel, and I saw to my dismay that there are so many kitchens, not kitchens that are established in order to serve caste restrictions, but kitchens that have become necessary in order that we can have condiments and the exact weight of condiments, to which we were used in the respective countries or the places or Provinces from which we have come. For the Brahmanas themselves there are different compartments and different kitchens catering after the delicate tastes of those different groups. I suggest to you that this is simply slavery to the palate rather than mastery of the palate. Unless we are satisfied with foods that are necessary for the proper maintenance of our physical health, and unless we are prepared to rid ourselves of those stimulating and heating and exciting condiments that we mix with our food, we will certainly not be able to control the over-abundant unnecessary exciting energy that we may have. Eating and drinking and indulging in passion, we share in common with the animals, but have you seen a horse, a cow indulging in palate to the excess that we do? Do you suppose that it is a sign of civilisation, a sign of actual life that we should multiply our eatables so far that we do not know where we are?

VOW OF NON-THIEVING

The next rule is the vow of non-thieving. We are theives in a way if we take anything that we do not need for immediate use, and keep it from some body else who needs it. It is a fundamental law of Nature, that Nature produces enough for our wants from day to-day, and if only every body took only enough for him and no more, there will be no poverty in the world, and there will be no man dying of starvation in this world. And so long as we have got this inequality, so long I shall have to say we are thieves. I am no socialist, and I do not want to dispossess those who have got possessions, but I do say that personally those of us who want to see darkness out of light have to follow this doctrine. In India, we have three millions of people having to be satisfied with only one meal consisting of a chapati containing no fat in it and a pinch of salt.

VOW OF SWADESHI

The vow of Swadeshi is a necessary vow. I suggest to you that we are departing from one of the sacred laws of our being when we leave our neighbour and go somewhere else to satisfy our wants. If a man comes from Bombay here and offers you wares, you are not justified in supporting the Bombay merchant or trader so long as you have got a merchant at your very door born and bred in Madras. That is my view of Swadeshi, In your village, so long as you have a village barber, you are bound to support the village barber to the exclusion of the finished barber that may come to you from Madras. Train your village barber by all means to reach the attainment of the barber from Madras, but until he does so, you are not justified in going to the Madras barber. When we find that there are many things we cannot get, we try to do without them. We may have to do without so many things which to-day we consider necessary, and believe me when you have that frame of mind, you will find a great burden taken off your shoulders even as the pilgrim did in that inimitable book *Pilgrim's Progress.*

VOW OF FEARLESSNESS

I found through my wanderings in India that all educated India is seized with a paralysing fear. We may not open our lips in public. We may not declare our confirmed opinions in public. We may hold those opinions, and we may talk about them secretly, and we may do anything within the four walls of a house, but those opinions are not for public consumption. If we took a vow of silence, I would have nothing to say, but when we open our lips in public we say things which we really do not believe. I do not know whether this is not the experience of almost every one who speaks in public. I then suggest to you that there is only one Being, if Being is the proper term to be applied, whom we have to fear, and that is God. If you want to follow the vow of truth in any shape or form, fearlessness is the necessary consequence.

UNTOUCHABLES

We have also a vow in connection with the untouchables. There is an ineffaceable blot which Hinduism carries with it to-day. I have declined to believe that it has been handed to us from immemorial times. I think that these miserable, wretched, enslaving spirits of untouchables must have come to us when we were in a cycle of our lives at our lowest ebb, and that evil has stuck to us, and it remains with us. It is to my mind a curse that has come to us, and so long as it remains with us, we are bound to consider that every affliction that we labour under in this sacred land is a fit and proper punishment for the great crime that we are committing. That any person should be considered untouchable because of his calling passes one's comprehension, and you, the student world, who receive all this modern education, if you become a party to this crime, it were better that you receive no education whatsoever. We are labouring under a heavy handicap. You, although you may realise that there cannot be a single human being on this earth who should be considered to be untouchable, you cannot react upon your families and upon your surroundings, because all your thought is conceived in a foreign tongue. So we have introduced a rule in the Ashrama that we shall receive our education through the Vernaculars. In order to solve the problem of languages in India, we in the Ashrama make it a point of learning as many Indian Vernaculars as we possibly can, and I assure you that the trouble of learning these languages is nothing compared to the trouble that we have to take in mastering the English language. Even after all that trouble, it is not possible for us to express ourselves in the English language as clearly as in our own mother tongue. Education has enabled us to see the horrible crime in connection with the so-called untouchables, but we are seized with fear, and we have got our superstitious veneration for our family traditions and for the members of our families.

POLITICS

Last of all, when you have conformed to these rules, I think then, and not till then, you may come to politics and dabble in them to your heart's content. Politics divorced from religions, have absolutely no meaning, and if the student world crowd the political platforms of the country, to my mind, it is not necessarily a healthy sign of national growth; but that does not mean that we in student-life ought not to learn politics. Politics are also a part of our being. We want to understand our national institutions, we ought to understand our national growth. So, in the Ashrama, every child is taught to understand political institutions, and know how the country is vibrating with new emotions, with new aspirations, with new life; but we want also the infallible light of religious faith, not faith which merely appeals to the intelligence, but faith which is indelibly inscribed in the heart. To-day what happens is that immediately young men cease to be students they sink into oblivion, and they seek miserable employments, carrying miserable emoluments, knowing nothing of God, knowing nothing of fresh air and fresh light, and knowing nothing of that real vigorous independence that comes out of obedience to those laws that I have placed before you.

CONCLUSION

I am not here asking you to crowd into the Ashrama—there is no room there. But I say that every one of you may enact that Ashrama life individually and collectively. I shall be satisfied with anything that you may choose from the rules I have ventured to place before you and act up to it. But if you think that these are the outpourings of a mad man, you will not hesitate to tell me that it is so, and I shall take that judgment from you undismayed, (Loud cheers.)

SOCIAL SERVICE

[*The anniversary meeting of the* •*Social Service League, Madras,* (1916) *was held at the quadrangle of the Christian College, the Anderson Hall having been found insufficient to accommodate the immensely large gathering which had begun to assemble from an early hour. Mrs. Whitehead presided. Bishop Whitehead was also present. Mr. Gandhi having been called upon by Mrs. Whitehead to address the meeting said*] :—

For social service as for any other service on the face of this earth, there is one condition indispensable, *viz.*, proper qualifications on the part of those who want to render social service or any other service, and so we shall ask ourselves this evening whether those of us who are already engaged in this kind of service and those who aspire to render that service possess those necessary qualifications, because you will agree with me that servants if they can mend matters, they can also spoil matters, and in trying to do service, however well-intentioned that service might be, if they are not qualified for that service, they will be rendering not service but disservice.

THE SOCIAL SERVANT

What are those qualifications? I imagine I could almost repeat to you the qualifications that I described this morning to the students in the Y. M. C. A. Hall, because they are of universal application, and they are necessary for any class of work, and much more so in social service at this time of the day in our national life, in our dear country. It seems to me that we do require truth in the one hand and fearlessness in the other hand. Unless we carry the torchlight of truth we shall not see the state in front, and unless we carry the quality of fearlessness we shall not be able to give the message that we might want to give on proper occasions, when the occasion for testing us comes, and such occasions do not occur so often as they might imagine they come but rarely. They are special privileges, and unless we have this fearlessness, I feel sure that when that supreme final test comes we shall be found wanting; and then I ask, and I ask you to ask yourselves, whether those of you, who are engaged in this service and those of you, who want hereafter to engage in this service, have these two qualities. But let me remind you also that these two qualities may be trained in us in a manner detrimental to ourselves and in a manner detrimental to those with whom we may come in contact. That is a dangerous statement almost to make, but when I make that statement I would like you to consider that truth comes not as truth but only as truth so called. You will recall the instance of Ravana and Rama. You will recall the instance of Lakshmana on the one hand and Indrajit on the other in that inimitable book *Ramayana*. Both Lakshmana and Indrajit performed austerities, both of them had attained to a certain kind of self-control, and yet we find that what Indrajit possessed was as mere dross and that what Lakshman possessed was of great assistance and he has left a treasure for us to cherish and to value. What was that additional quality that Lakshmana possessed ? I venture to suggest to you that Lakshmana was divinely guided, that he had religious perception and that his life was guided upon principle and based upon religion, while, that of Indrajit was based upon irreligion. Life without religion, I hold, is life without principle, and life without principle, is like a ship without a rudder; and just as a ship without a rudder will be tossed about from place to place, and never reach its destination, so will a man without this religious backing, without that hard grasp of religion be also tossed about on this stormy ocean of the world, without ever reaching his destined goal. And so I suggest to every social servant that he may not run away with the idea that he will serve his fellow-countrymen unless he got those two qualities duly sanctified by religious perception, by a life so far divinely guided.

VILLAGE SANITATION

Our Chair Lady was good enough to take me to a village that is just behind the compound of the Bishop's house. It is a Pariah village. She described to me the condition that little village was in before this League commenced its operations there, and I am an eyewitness to what that village is to-day, and I make myself bold to state that that village is a model of cleanliness and order, and it is certainly much cleaner than some of the busiest and the most central parts of Madras. That is an undoubtedly creditable piece of work on the part of the Social Service League, and if the League can penetrate into the recesses of Madras and do the same kind of work, the things which I have noticed in Madras will be conspicuous by their absence when I next pay my visit to this great city. It is not enough that we clean out the villages occupied by our Pariah brethren. If they are amenable to reason, to persuasion, shall we have to say that the so-called highest classes are not equally amenable to reason, to persuasion and are not amenable to the hygenic laws which are indispensable in order to live a city life? We may do many things with impunity when we have got vast acres of open ground to surround us, but when we transport ourselves to crowded streets where we have hardly air space enough to give our lungs the proper quantity of air, the life becomes changed and we have to obey another set of laws.

It is no use saddling the Municipality with responsibility for the conditions in which we find not only the central parts of Madras, but the conditions in which we find the central parts of every city in India without exception —and I have gone now to almost every city of importance in India. I feel that no Municipality in the world will be able to override the habits that a class of people may have in them, and have been handed down to them from generation to generation. It is work that can be done only by patient toil and guidance, with those two immutable weapons in our hands. It can be done only by such bodies as a Social Service League. If we are pulsating with the new life, with the new vision which shall open before us in the near future, I think there are signs which will be an indication to show that we are pulsating with a new life which is going to be a proper life for us, which will add dignity to our Nationality and which will carry the banner of progress forward. I therefore suggest to you that the question of sanitary reform in this big city is practically a hopeless task if we expect our Municipality to do it unaided by this voluntary work. Far be it from me to absolve the Municipality from their responsibility. I think that there is still a great deal left to be done by the Municipality.

BENARES

Mr. Gandhi then proceeded to deal with the great need for the work of a Social Service League in such a sacred city as Benares, where there was a mass of dirt and confusion and want of orderliness so much detrimental to the preservation of the holiness and sanctity of the place. What was true of the Kashi temple was true of a majority of their Hindu temples. Such problems could not be solved so successfully by the Government or Municipality as by voluntary bodies like the Social Service League. Those who took up League work ought to be nurtured in new traditions. They were filled with horror at many evils they witnessed, and that was a position that stared Social Service Leagues in the face throughout the length and breadth of India.

SCHOOL AND FAMILY LIFE

Much of the neglect of such work, Mr. Gandhi pointed out, was due to the condition of the country at present, when the school life was not an extension of family life, and if that were so, students would respond and analyse the difficulties that faced them and they would still be going to temples while they were at the same time visiting temples. Before students could take up such work in this country, the educational system would have to be revolutionalised. They were to-day in a hopelessly false position, and they would incur the curse of the next generation for the great tragedy they saw being enacted before them to-day. It was a matter for thinking and it was a matter for redressing, no matter how difficult of attainment the result might be to-day. The task was herculean, but if the task was herculean the reward that they would receive from the blessings of generations to come would be an adequate reward.

The lecturer then dealt with the need for work on the part of Social Service Leagues in order to ameliorate the condition of third class passengers in railway carriages, so as to minimise overcrowding, discomfort and fatigue and what not.

In conclusion the lecturer said that if those who undertook social service would carry courage with them wherever they went, their efforts would be crowned with success.

SWADESHI

[*A Paper read before the Missionary Conference, Madras,* 1916.]

It was not without much diffidence that I undertook to speak to you at all. And I was hard put to it in the selection of my subject. I have chosen a very delicate and difficult subject. It is delicate because of the peculiar views I hold upon Swadeshi, and it is difficult because I have not that command of language which is necessary for giving adequate expression to my thoughts. I know that I may rely upon your indulgence for the many shortcomings you will no doubt find in my address, the more so when I tell you that there is nothing in what I am about to say that I am not either already practising or am not preparing to practise to the best of my ability. It encourages me to observe that last month you devoted a week to prayer in the place of an address. I have earnestly prayed that what I am about to say may bear fruit, and I know that you will bless my word with a similar prayer.

After much thinking I have arrived at a definition of Swadeshi that perhaps best illustrates my meaning. Swadeshi is that spirit in us which restricts us to the use and service of our immediate surroundings to the exclusion of the more remote. Thus, as for religion, in order to satisfy the requirements of the definition, I must restrict myself to my ancestral religion. That is the use of my immediate religious surrounding. If I find it defective I should serve it by purging it of its defects. In the domain of politics I should make use of the indigenous institutions and serve them by curing them of their proved defects. In that of economics I should use only things that are produced by my immediate neighbours and serve those industries by making them efficient and complete where they might be found wanting. It is suggested that such Swadeshi, if reduced to practice, will lead to the millennium. And as we do not abandon our pursuit after the millennium because we do not expect quite to reach it within our times, so may we not abandon Swadeshi even though it may not be fully attained for generations to come.

Let us briefly examine the three branches of Swadeshi as sketched above. Hinduism has become a conservative religion and therefore a mighty force because of the Swadeshi spirit underlying it. It is the most tolerant because it is non-proselytising, and it is as capable of expansion to-day as it has been found to be in the past. It has succeeded not in driving, as I think it has been erroneously held, but in absorbing Buddhism. By reason of the Swadeshi spirit a Hindu refuses to change his religion not necessarily because he considers it to be the best, but because he knows that he can complement it by introducing reforms. And what I have said about Hinduism is, I suppose, true of the other great faiths of the world, only it is held that it is specially so in the case of Hinduism. But here comes the point I am labouring to reach. If there is any substance in what I have said, will not the great missionary bodies of India, to whom she owes a deep debt of gratitude for what they have done and are doing, do still better and serve the spirit of Christianity better by dropping the goal of proselytising but continuing their philanthropic work? I hope you will not consider this to be an impertinence on my part. I make the suggestion in all sincerity and with due humility. Moreover, I have some claim upon your attention. I have endeavoured to study the Bible. I consider it as part of my scriptures. The spirit of the Sermon on the Mount competes almost on equal terms with the Bhagavad-Gita for the domination of my heart. I yield to no Christian in the strength of devotion with which I sing " Lead kindly light " and several other inspired hymns of a similar nature. I have come under the influence of noted Christian missionaries belonging to different denominations. And I enjoy to this day the privilege of friendship with some of them. You will, perhaps, therefore allow that I have offered the above suggestion not as a biased Hindu but as a humble and impartial student of religion with great leanings towards Christianity. May it not be that "Go Ye Unto All The World" message has been somewhat narrowly interpreted and the spirit of it missed? It will not be denied, I speak from experience, that many of the conversions are only so-called. In some cases the appeal has gone not to the heart but to the stomach. And in every case a conversion leaves a sore behind it which, I venture to think, is avoidable. Quoting again from experience, a new birth, a change of heart, is perfectly possible in every one of the great faiths. I know I am now treading upon thin ice. But I do not apologise, in closing this part of my subject, for saying that the frightful outrage that is just going on in Europe, perhaps, shows that the message of Jesus of Nazareth, the Son of Peace, had been little understood in Europe, and that light upon it may have to be thrown from the East.

I have sought your help in religious matters, which it is yours to give in a special sense. But I make bold to seek it even in political matters. I do not believe that religion has nothing to do with politics. The latter, divorced from religion, is like a corpse only fit to be buried. As a matter of fact in your own silent manner you influence politics not a little. And I feel that if the attempt to separate politics from religion had not been made as it is even now made, they would not have degenerated as they often appear to do. No one considers that the political life of the country is in a happy state. Following out the Swadeshi spirit I observe the indigenous institutions and the village panchayats hold me. India is really a republican country, and it is because it is that that it has survived every shock hitherto delivered. Princes and potentates, whether they were Indian born or foreigners, have hardly touched the vast masses except for collecting revenue. The latter in their turn seem to have rendered unto Cæsar's what was Cæsar's and for the rest have done much as they have liked. The vast organisation of caste answered not only the religious wants of the community, but it answered too its political needs. The villagers managed their internal affairs through the caste system, and through it they dealt with any oppression from the ruling power or powers. It is not possible to deny of a nation that was capable of producing the caste system its wonderful power of organisation. One had but to attend the great Kumbha Mela at Hardwar last year to know how skilful that organisation must have been, which, without any seeming effort, was able effectively to cater for more than a million pilgrims. Yet it is the fashion to say that we lack organising ability. This is true, I fear, to a certain extent, of those who have been nurtured in the new traditions. We have laboured under a terrible handicap owing to an almost fatal departure from the Swadeshi spirit. We, the educated classes, have received our education through a foreign tongue. We have therefore, not reacted upon the masses. We want to represent the masses, but we fail. They recognise us not much more than they recognise the English officers. Their hearts are an open book to neither. Their aspirations are not ours. Hence there is a break. And you witness not in reality failure to organise but want of correspondence between the representatives and the represented. If, during the last fifty years, we had been educated through the vernaculars, our elders and our servants and our neighbours would have partaken of our knowledge; the discoveries of a Bose or a Ray would have been household treasures as are the Ramayan and the Mahabharat. As it is, so far as the masses are concerned, those great discoveries might as well have been made by foreigners. Had instruction in all the branches of learning been given through the Vernaculars, I make bold to say that they would have been enriched wonderfully. The question of village sanitation, etc., would have been solved long ago. The village Pancha yats would be now a living force in a special way, and India would almost be enjoying Self-Government suited to its requirements and would have been spared the humiliating spectacle of organised assassination on its sacred soil. It is not too late to mend. And you can help if you will, as no other body or bodies can.

And now for the last division of Swadeshi. Much of the deep poverty of the masses is due to the ruinous departure from Swadeshi in the economic and industrial life. If not an article of commerce had been brought from outside India, she would be to-day a land flowing with milk and honey. But that was not to be. We were greedy and so was England. The connection between England and India was based clear upon an error. But she does not remain in India in error. It is her declared policy that India is to be held in trust for her people. If this be true, Lancashire must stand aside. And if the Swadeshi doctrine is a sound doctrine, Lancashire can stand aside without hurt, though it may sustain a shock for the time being. I think of Swadeshi not as a boycott movement undertaken by way of revenge. I conceive it as a religious principle to be followed by all. I am no economist, but I have read some treatises which show that England could easily become a self-sustained country, growing all the produce she needs. This may be an utterly ridiculous proposition, and perhaps the best proof that it cannot be true is that England is one of the largest importers in the world. But India cannot live for Lancashire or any other country before she is able to live for herself. And she can live for herself only if she produces and is helped to produce every thing for her requirements within her own borders. She need not be, she ought not to be, drawn into the vortex of mad and ruinous competition which breeds fratricide, jealousy and many other evils. But who is to stop her great millionaries from entering into the world competition? Certainly not legislation. Force of public opinion, proper education, however, can do a great deal in the desired direction. The hand-loom industry is in a dying condition. I took special care during my wanderings last year to see as many weavers as possible, and my heart ached to find how they had lost, how families had retired from this one flourishing and honourable occupation. If we follow the Swadeshi doctrine, it would be your duty and mine to find out neighbours who can supply our wants and to teach them to supply them where they do not know how to, assuming that there are neighbours who are in want of healthy occupation. Then every village of India will almost be a self-supporting and self-contained unit, exchanging only such necessary commodities with other villages where they are not locally producible. This may all sound nonsensical. Well, India is a country of nonsense. It is nonsensical to parch one's throat with thirst when a kindly Muhammadan is ready to offer pure water to drink. And yet thousands of Hindus would rather die of thirst than drink water from a Muhammadan household. These nonsensical men can also, once they are convinced that their religion demands that they should wear garments manufactured in India only and eat food only grown in India, decline to wear any other clothing or eat any other food. Lord Curzon set the fashion for tea-drinking. And that pernicious drug now bids fair to overwhelm the nation. It has already undermined the digestive apparatus of hundreds of thousands of men and women and constitutes an additional tax upon their slender purses. Lord

Hardinge can set the fashion for Swadeshi and almost the whole of India will forswear foreign goods. There is a verse in the Bhagavat Gita which, freely rendered, means masses follow the classes. It is easy to undo the evil if the thinking portion of the community were to take the Swadeshi vow, even though it may for a time cause considerable inconvenience. I hate legislative interference in any department of life. At best it is the lesser evil. But I would tolerate, welcome, indeed plead for a stiff protective duty upon foreign goods. Natal, a British colony, protected its sugar by taxing the sugar that came from another British colony, Mauritius. England has sinned against India by forcing free trade upon her. It may have been food for her, but it has been poison for this country.

It has often been urged that India cannot adopt Swadeshi in the economic life at any rate. Those who advance this objection do not look upon Swadeshi as a rule of life. With them it is a mere patriotic effort not to be made if it involved any self-denial. Swadeshi, as defined here, is a religious discipline to be undergone in utter disregard of the physical discomfort it may cause to individuals. Under its spell the deprivation of a pin or a needle, because these are not manufactured in India, need cause no terror. A Swadeshist will learn to do without hundreds of things which to-day he considers necessary. Moreover, those who dismiss the Swadeshi from their minds by arguing the impossible forget that Swadeshi, after all, is a goal to be reached by steady effort. And we would be making for the goal even if we confined Swadeshi to a given set of articles allowing ourselves as a temporary measure to use such things as might not be procurable in the country.

There now remains for me to consider one more objection that has been raised against Swadeshi. The objectors consider it to be a most selfish doctrine without any warrant in the civilised code of morality. With them to practise Swadeshi is to revert to barbarism. I cannot enter into a detailed analysis of the proposition. But I would urge that Swadeshi is the only doctrine consistent with the law of humility and love. It is arrogance to think of launching out to serve the whole of India when I am hardly able to serve even my own family. It were better to concentrate my effort upon the family and consider that through them I was serving the whole nation and if you will the whole of humanity. This is humility and it is love. The motive will determine the quality of the act. I may serve my family regardless of the sufferings I may cause to others, as for instance, I may accept an employment which enables me to extort money from people, I enrich myself thereby and then satisfy many unlawful demands of the family. Here I am neither serving the family nor the State. Or I may recognise that God has given me hands and feet only to work with for my sustenance and for that of those who may be dependent upon me. I would then at once simplify my life and that of those whom I can directly reach. In this instance I would have served the family without causing injury to anyone else. Supposing that every one followed this mode of life, we would have at once an ideal state. All will not reach that state at the same time. But those of us who, realising its truth, enforce it in practice will clearly anticipate and accelerate the coming of that happy day. Under this plan of life, in seeming to serve India to the exclusion of every other country, I do not harm any other country. My patriotism is both exclusive and inclusive. It is exclusive in the sense that in all humility I confine my attention to the land of my birth, but it is inclusive in the sense that my service is not of a competitive or antagonistic nature. *Sic utere tuo ut alienum non leedas* is not merely a legal maxim, but it is a grand doctrine of life. It is the key to a proper practice of *Ahimsa* or love. It is for you, the custodians of a great faith, to set the fashion and show by your preaching, sanctified by practice, that patriotism based on "hatred killeth" and that patriotism based on "love giveth life."

ECONOMIC *vs.* MORAL PROGRESS

[*Mr. M. K. Gandhi delivered an instructive lecture on " Does economic progress clash with real progress?" at a meeting of the Muir Central College Economic Society held in the Physical Science Theatre. The Hon. Pandit Madan Mohan Malaviya presided*] :—

When I accepted Mr. Kapildeva Malaviya's invitation to speak to you upon the subject of this evening, I was painfully conscious of my limitations. You are an economic society. You have chosen distinguished specialists for the subjects included in your syllabus for this year and the next. I seem to be the only speaker ill-fitted for the task set before him. Frankly and truly, I know very little of economics, as you naturally understand them. Only the other day, sitting at an evening meal, a civilian friend deluged me with a series of questions on my crankisms. As he proceeded in his cross-examination, I being a willing victim, he found no difficulty in discovering my gross ignorance of the matters I appeared to him to be handling with a cocksuredness worthy only of a man who knows not that he knows not. To his horror and even indignation, I suppose, he found that I had not even read books on economics by such well-known authorities as Mill, Marshall, Adam Smith and a host of such other authors. In despair, he ended by advising me to read these works before experimenting in matters economic at the expense of the public. He little knew that I was a sinner past redemption. My experiments continue at the expense of trusting friends. For there come to us moments in life when about somethings we need no proof from without. A little voice within us tells, "you are on the right track, move neither to your left nor right, but keep to the straight and narrow way." With such help we march forward slowly indeed, but surely and steadily. That is my position. It may be satisfactory enough for me, but it can in no way answer the requirements of a society such as yours. Still it was no use my struggling against Mr. Kapildeva Malaviya. I knew that he was intent upon having me to engage your attention for one of your evenings. Perhaps you will treat my intrusion as a welcome diversion from the trodden path. An occasional fast after a series of sumptuous feasts is often a necessity. And as with the body so, I imagine, is the case with the reason. And if your reason this evening is found fasting instead of feasting, I am sure it will enjoy with the greater avidity the feast that Rao Bahadur Pandit Chaddrika Prasad has in store for you for the 12th of January.

Before I take you to the field of my experiences and experiments it is perhaps best to have a mutual understanding about the title of this evening's address. Does economic progress clash with real progress? By economic progress, I take it, we mean material advancement without limit and by real progress we mean moral progress, which again is the same thing as progress of the permanent element in us. The subject may therefore be stated thus: Does not moral progress increase in the same proportion as material progress? I know that this is a wider proposition than the one before us. But I venture to think that we always mean the larger one even when we lay down the smaller. For we know enough of science to realise that there is no such thing as perfect rest or repose in this visible universe of ours. If therefore material progress does not clash with moral progress it must necessarily advance the latter. Nor can we be satisfied with the clumsy way in which sometimes those who cannot defend the larger proposition put their case. They seem to be obsessed with the concrete case of thirty millions of India stated by the late Sir William Wilson Hunter to be living on one meal a day. They say that before we can think or talk of their moral welfare we must satisfy their daily wants. With these, they say, material progress spells moral progress. And then is taken a sudden jump: what is true of thirty millions is true of the universe. They forget that hard cases make bad law. I need hardly say to you how ludicrously absurd this deduction would be. No one has ever suggested that grinding pauperism can lead to anything else than moral degradation. Every human being has a right to live, and therefore to find the where withal to feed himself and, where necessary, to clothe and house himself. But for this very simple performance we need no assistance from economists or their laws.

"Take no thought for the morrow" is an injunction which finds an echo in almost all the religious scriptures of the world. In well-ordered society the securing of one's livelihood should be and is found to be the easiest thing in the world. Indeed the test of orderliness in a country is not the number of millionaires it owns, but the absence of starvation among its masses. The only statement that has to be examined is whether it can be laid down as a law of universal application that material advancement means moral progress.

Now let us take a few illustrations. Rome suffered a moral fall when it attained high material affluence. So did Egypt, and so perhaps most countries of which we have any historical record. The descendants and kinsmen of the royal and divine Krishna too fell when they were rolling in riches. We do not deny to the Rocksfellers and the Carnegies possession of an ordinary measure of morality but we gladly judge them indulgently. I mean that we do not even expect them to satisfy the highest standard of morality. With them material gain has not necessarily meant moral gain. In South Africa where I had the privilege of associating with thousands of our countrymen on most intimate terms, I observed almost invariably that the greater the possession of riches the greater was their moral turpitude. Our rich men, to say the least, did not advance the moral struggle of passive resistance as did the poor. The rich men's sense of self respect was not so much injured as that of the poorest. If I were not afraid of treading on dangerous ground, I would even come nearer home, and show you that possession of riches has been a hindrance to real growth. I venture to think that the scriptures of the world are far safer and sounder treatises on laws of economics than many of the modern text-books. The question we are asking ourselves this evening is not a new one. It was addressed to Jesus two thousand years ago. St. Mark has vividly described the scene. Jesus is in his solemn mood; he is earnest. He talks of eternity. He knows the world about him. He is himself the greatest economist of his time. He succeeded in economising time and space—he transcended them. It is to him at his best that one comes running, kneels down, and asks: "Good Master, what shall I do that I may inherit eternal life?" And Jesus said unto him: 'Why callest thou me good? There is none good but one, that is, God. Thou knowest the commandments. Do not commit adultery, Do not kill, Do not steal, Do not bear false witness, Defraud not, Honour thy father and mother.' And he answered and said unto him: 'Master, all these have I observed from my youth.' Then Jesus beholding him loved him and said unto him: 'One thing thou lackest. Go thy way, sell whatever thou hast and give to the poor, and thou shall have treasure in heaven—come take up the cross and follow me.' And he was sad at that saying and went away grieved—for he had great possessions. And Jesus looked round about and said unto his disciples: 'How hardly shall they that have riches enter into the kingdom of God.' And the disciples were astonished at his words. But Jesus answereth again and saith unto them 'Children, how hard is it for them that trust in riches to enter into the kingdom of God. It is easier for a camel to go through the eye of a needle than for a rich man to enter into the kingdom of God!" Here you have an eternal rule of life stated in the noblest words the English language is capable of producing. But the disciples nodded unbelief as we do even to this day. To him they said as we say to day: But look how the law fails in practice. If we sell all and have nothing we shall have nothing to eat. We must have money or we cannot even be reasonably moral. So they state their case thus! "And they were astonished out of measure, saying among themselves: 'Who then can be saved'. And Jesus looking upon them saith: 'With men it is impossible but not with God, for with God all things are possible'. Then Peter began to say unto him: 'Lo, we have left all, and have followed thee.' And Jesus answered and said: 'Verily I say unto you there is no man that has left house or brethren or sisters, or father or mother, or wife or children or lands for my sake and the Gospel's but he shall receive one hundredfold now in this time houses and brethren and sisters and mothers and children and lands with persecutions, and in the world to come eternal life. But many that are first shall be last and the last first.'" You have here the result or reward, if you prefer the term, of following the law. I have not taken the trouble of copying similar passages from the other non-Hindu scriptures and I will not insult you by quoting in support of the law stated by Jesus passages from the writings and sayings of our own sages, passages even stronger if possible than the Biblical extracts. I have drawn your attention to, perhaps the strongness of all the testimonies in favour of the affirmative answer to the question before us are the lives of the greatest teachers of the world. Jesus, Mahomed, Buddba, Nanak, Kabir, Chaitanya, Sankara, Dayanand, Ramakrishna were men who exercised an immense influence over and moulded the character of thousands of men. The world is the richer for their having lived in it. And they were all men who deliberately embraced poverty as their lot.

I should not have laboured my point as I have done, if I did not believe that, in so far as we have made the modern materialistic craze our goal, in so far are we going down hill in the path of progress. I hold that economic progress in the sense I have put it is antagonistic to real progress. Hence the ancient ideal has been the limitation of activities promoting wealth. This does not put an end to all material ambition. We should still have as we have always had in our midst people who make the pursuit of wealth their aim in life. But we have always recognised that it is a fall from the ideals. It is a beautiful thing to know that the wealthiest among us have often felt that to have remained voluntarily poor would have been a higher state for them. That you cannot serve God and Mammon is an economic truth of the highest value. We have to make our choice. Western Nations are to day groaning under the heel of the monster god of materialism. Their moral growth has become stunted. They measure their progress in £ *s. d.* American wealth has become the standard. She is the envy of the other Nations. I have heard many of our countrymen say that we will gain American wealth but avoid its method. I venture to suggest that such an attempt if it were made is foredoomed to failure. We cannot be " wise, temperate and furious " in a moment. I would have our leaders to teach us to be morally supreme in the world. This land of ours was once, we are told, the abode of the Gods. It is not possible to conceive Gods inhabiting a land which is made hideous by the smoke and the din of mill chimneys and factories and whose road ways are traversed by rushing engines dragging numerous cars crowded with men mostly who know not what they are after, who are often absent minded, and whose tempers do not improve by being uncomfortably packed like sardines in boxes and finding themselves in the midst of utter strangers who would oust them if they could and, whom they would in their turn oust similarly. I refer to these things because they are held to be symbolical of material progress. But they add not an atom to our happiness. This is what Wallace, the great scientist, has said as his deliberate judgment. "In the earliest records which have come down to us from the past, we find ample indications that general ethical considerations and conceptions, the accepted standard of morality, and the conduct resulting from these, were in no degree inferior to those which prevail to-day." In a series of chapters he then proceeds to examine the position of the English Nation under the advance in wealth it has made. He says: "This rapid growth of wealth and increase of our power over nature put too great a strain upon our crude civilization, on our superficial Christianity, and it was accompanied by various forms of social immorality almost as amazing and unprecedented." He then shows how factories have risen on the corpses of men, women and children, how as-the country has rapidly advanced in riches it has gone down in morality. He shows this by dealing with insanitation, life destroying trades, adulteration, bribery, and gambling. He shows how with the advance of wealth justice has become immoral, deaths from alcoholism and suicide have increased, the average of premature births and congenital defects has increased and prostitution has become an institution. He concludes his examination by these pregnant remarks:

" The proceedings of the divorce courts show other aspects of the result of wealth and leisure while a friend who had been a good deal in London society assured me that both in country houses and in London various kinds of orgies were occasionally to be met with which would hardly have been surpassed in the period of the most dissolute Emperors. O War, too, I need say nothing. It has always been more or less chronic since the rise of the Roman Empire; but there is now undoubtedly a disinclination for war among all civilized peoples. Yet the vast burden of armaments taken together with the most pious declarations in favour of peace, must be held to show an almost total absence of morality as a guiding principle among the governing classes."

Under the British aegis we have learnt much, but it is my firm belief that there is little to gain from Britain's intrinsic morality that if we are not careful, we shall introduce all the vices that she has been a prey to, owing to the disease of materialism. We can profit by that connection only if we keep our civilisation, and our morals straight, *i.e.*, if instead of boasting of the glorious past, we express the ancient moral glory in our own lives and let our lives bear witness to our past. Then we shall benefit her and ourselves. If we copy her because she provides us with rulers, both they and we shall suffer degradation. We need not be afraid of ideals or of reducing them to practice even to the uttermost. Ours will only then be a truly spiritual nation when we shall show more truth than gold, greater fearlessness than pomp of power and wealth, greater charity than love of self. If we will but clean our houses, our palaces and temples of the attributes of wealth and show in them the attributes of morality, we can offer battle to any combinations of hostile forces without having to carry the burden of a heavy militia. Let us seek first the Kingdom of God and His righteousness and the irrevocable promise is that everything will be added to us. These are real economics. May you and I treasure them and enforce them in our daily life.

EDUCATION ANCIENT AND MODERN

[Mr. Gandhi addressed in Hindi a public meeting at Allahabad at Munshi Ram Prasad's garden under the chairmanship of the Hon. Pandit Madan Mohan Malaviya. The gathering was a record one even for Munshi Ram Prasad's garden where some of the largest public meetings have been held] :—

Mr. Gandhi who on rising was greeted with loud and prolonged cheers, said that that he should have felt difficulty—of which he was ashamed—in addressing the meeting in Hindi was a striking commentary on the system of modern education which was a part of the subject of his lecture that evening. He would, however, prefer to speak in Hindi although he had greater facility of expression in English. Describing the modern system of education he said that real education was considered to have begun at the college at the age of 16 or 17. The education received in school was not useful. For instance, an Indian student, while he knew well the geography of England, did not possess a sufficient knowledge of the geography of his own country. The history of India which they were taught was greatly distorted. Government service was the aim of their education. Their highest ambition was to become members of the Imperial Legislative Council. The boys abandoned their hereditary occupations, and forsook their mother tongue. They were adopting the English language, European ideas and European dress. They thought in English, conducted all their political and social work and all commercial transactions, etc., in English and thought that they could not do without the English language. They had come to think that there was no other road. Education through English had created a wide gulf between the educated few and the masses. It had created a gulf in the families also. An English educated man had no community of feelings and ideas with the ladies of his family. And, as had been said, the aspirations of the English educated men were fixed on Government service and at the most on membership of the Imperial Legislative Council. He for one could never commend a system of education which produced such a state of things and men educated under such system could not be expected to do any great service to the country. Mr. Gandhi did not mean that the English educated leaders did not feel for the masses. On the other hand, he acknowledged that the Congress and other great public movements were initiated and conducted by them. But, at the same time, he could not help feeling that the work done during all these years would have been much more and much greater progress would have been made if they had been taught in their mother tongue. It was unfortunate, said the speaker, that a feeling had come over them that there was no path to progress other than that which was being followed. They found themselves helpless. But it was not manliness to assume an attitude of helplessness.

Mr. Gandhi then described the ancient system of education and said that even elementary education imparted by the village teacher taught the student all that was necessary for their occupations. Those who went in for higher education became fully conversant with the science of wealth *Artha Sastra*, ethics and religion *Dharma Sastra.* In ancient times there were no restrictions on education. It was not controlled by the State but was solely in the hands of Brahmans who shaped the system of education solely with an eye to the welfare of the people. It was based on restraint and *Brahmacharya*. It was due to such a system of education that Indian civilization had outlived so many vicissitudes through thousands of years, while such ancient civilization as those of Greece, Rome and Egypt had become extinct. No doubt the wave of a new civilization had been passing through India. But he was sure that it was transitory, it would soon pass away and Indian civilization would be revivified. In ancient times the basis of life was self-restraint but now it was enjoyment. The result was that people had become powerless cowards and forsook the truth. Having come under the influence of another civilization it might be necessary to adapt our own civilization in certain respect to our new environments, but we should not make any radical change in a civilization which was acknowledged even by some western scholars to be the best. It might be urged that it was necessary to adopt the methods and instruments of western civilization to meet the material forces of that civilization. But the forces born of spirituality, the bed-rock of

Indian civilization, were more than a match for material forces. India was pre-eminently the land of religion. It was the first and the last duty of Indians to maintain it as such. They should draw their strength from the Soul, from God. If they adhered to that path Swarajya which they were aspiring to and working for would become their hand-maid.

THE MORAL BASIS OF CO-OPERATION

[*At the* 1917 *session of the Co-operative Conference held at Bombay, Mr. Gandhi introduced a paper on "The Moral Basis of Co-operation." The paper reads as follows*] :—

YOUR EXCELLENCY,—The only claim I have on your indulgence is that some months ago I attended with Mr. Ewbank a meeting of millhands to whom he wanted to explain the principles of co-operation. The chawl in which they were living was as filthy as it well could be. Recent rains had made matters worse. And I must frankly confess that had it not been for Mr. Ewbank's great zeal for the cause he has made his own, I should have shirked the task. But there we were, seated on a fairly worn out *charpai*, surrounded by men, women and children. Mr. Ewbank opened fire on a man who had put himself forward and who wore not a particularly innocent countenance. After he had engaged him and the other people about him in Gujarati conversation, he wanted me to speak to the people. Owing to the suspicious looks of the man who was first spoken to, I naturally pressed home the moralities of co-operation. I fancy that Mr. Ewbank rather liked the manner in which I handled the subject. Hence, I believe, his kind invitation to me to tax your patience for a few moments upon a consideration of co-operation from a moral standpoint.

My knowledge of the technicality of co-operation is next to nothing. My brother Devdhar has made the subject his own. Whatever he does, naturally attracts me and predisposes me to think that there must be something good in it and the handling of it must be fairly difficult. Mr. Ewbank very kindly placed at my disposal some literature too on the subject. And I have had a unique opportunity of watching the effect of some co-operative effect in Champaran. I have gone through Mr. Ewbank's ten main points which are like the commandments, and I have gone through the twelve points of Mr. Collins of Behar, which remind me of the law of the twelve tables. There are so-called agricultural banks in Champaran. They were to me disappointing efforts, if they were meant to be demonstrations of the success of co-operation. On the other hand, there is quiet work in the same direction being done by Mr. Hodge, a missionary whose efforts are leaving their impress on those who come in contact with him. Mr. Hodge is a co-operative enthusiast and probably considers that the results which he sees flowing from his efforts are due to the working of co-operation. I who was able to watch the two efforts had no hesitation in inferring that the personal equation counted for success in the one and failure in the other instance.

I am an enthusiast myself, but twenty-five years of experimenting and experience have made me a cautious and discriminating enthusiast. Workers in a cause necessarily, though quite unconsciously, exaggerate its merits and often succeed in turning its very defects into advantages. In spite of my caution I consider the little institution I am conducting in Ahmedabad as the finest thing in the world. It alone gives me sufficient inspiration. Critics tell me that it represents a soulless soul-force and that its severe discipline has made it merely mechanical. I suppose both—the critics and I—are wrong. It is, at best, a humble attempt to place, at the disposal of the nation, a home where men and women may have scope for free and unfettered development of character, in keeping with the national genius, and if its controllers do not take care, the discipline that is the foundation of character may frustrate the very end in view. I would venture, therefore, to warn enthusiasts in co-operation against entertaining false hopes.

With Sir Daniel Hamilton it has become a religion. On the 13 January last he addressed the students of the Scottish Churches College, and in order to point a moral he instanced Scotland's poverty of two hundred years ago and showed how that great country was raised from a condition of poverty to plenty. " There were two powers," he said, " which raised her —the Scottish Church and the Scottish banks. The Church manufactured the men and the banks manufactured the money to give the men a start in life . . . . The Church disciplined the nation in the fear of God which is the beginning of wisdom and in the parish schools of the Church the children learned that the chief end of man's life was to glorify God and to enjoy Him forever. . . . Men were trained to believe in God and in themselves and on the trustworthy character so created the Scottish banking system was built." Sir Daniel then shows that it was possible to build up the marvellous Scottish banking system only on the character so built. So far there can only be perfect agreement with Sir Daniel, for without character there is no co-operation is a sound maxim. But he would have us go much further. He thus waxes eloquent on co-operation: "Whatever may be your day dreams of India's future never forget this that it is to weld India into one, and so enable her to take her rightful place in the world, that the British Government is here; and the welding hammer in the hand of the Government is the co-operative movement." In his opinion it is the panacea of all the evils that afflict India at the present moment. In its extended sense it can justify the claim on one condition which need not be mentioned here; in the limited sense in which Sir Daniel has used it, I venture to think, it is an enthusiast's exaggeration. Mark his peroration: "Credit, which is only Trust and Faith, is becoming more and more the money power of the world, and in the parchment bullet into which is impressed the faith which removes mountains, India will find victory and peace." Here there is evident confusion of thought. The credit which is becoming the money power of the world has little moral basis and is not synonym for Trust or Faith which are purely moral qualities. After twenty year's experience of hundreds of men, who had dealings with banks in South Africa, the opinion I had so often heard expressed has become firmly rooted in me, that the greater the rascal the greater the credit he enjoys with his banks. The banks do not pry into his moral character: they are satisfied that he meets his overdrafts and promissory notes punctually. The credit system has encircled this beautiful globe of ours like a serpent's coil, and if we do not mind, it bids fair to crush us out of breath. I have witnessed the ruin of many a home through the system, and it has made no difference whether the credit was labelled co-operative or otherwise. The deadly coil has made possible the devastating spectacle in Europe, which we are helplessly looking on. It was perhaps never so true as it is to-day that as in law so in war the longest purse finally wins. I have ventured to give prominence to the current belief about credit system in order to emphasize the point that the co-operative movement will be a blessing to India only to the extent that it is a moral movement strictly directed by men fired with religious fervour. It follows, therefore that co-operation should be confined to men wishing to be morally right, but failing to do so, because of grinding poverty or of the grip of the Mahajan. Facility for obtaining loans at fair rates will not make immoral or unmoral men moral. But the wisdom of the state or philanthropists demands that they should help, on the onward path, men struggling to be good.

Too often do we believe that material prosperity means moral growth. It is necessary that a movement which is fraught with so much good to India should not degenerate into one for merely advancing cheap loans. I was therefore delighted to read the recommendation in the Report of the Committee on Co-operation in India, that "they wish clearly to express their opinion that it is to true co-operation alone, that is, to a co-operation which recognises the moral aspect of the question, that Government must look for the amelioration of the masses and not to a pseudo-co-operative edifice, however imposing, which is built in ignorance of co-operative principles. With this standard before us, we will not measure the success of the movement by the number of co-operative societies formed, but by the moral condition of the co-operators. The Registrars will in that event ensure the moral growth of existing societies before multiplying them. And the Government will make their promotion conditional, not upon the number of societies they have registered, but the moral success of the existing institutions. This will mean tracing the course of every *pice* lent to the members. Those responsible for the proper conduct of co-operative societies will see to it that the money advanced does not find its way into the toddy-seller's till or into the pockets of the keepers of gambling dens. I would excuse the rapacity of the Mahajan if it has succeeded in keeping the gambling den or toddy from the ryot's home.

A word perhaps about the Mahajan will not be out of place. Co-operation is not a new device. The ryots co-operate to drum out monkeys or birds that destroy their crops. They co-operate to use a common threshing floor. I have found them co-operate to protect their cattle to the extent of their devoting their best land for the grazing of their cattle. And they have been found co-operating against a particularly rapacious Mahajan. Doubt has been expressed as to the success of co-operation because of the tightness of the Mahajan's hold on the ryots. I do not share the fears. The mightiest Mahajan must, if he represents an evil force, bend before co-operation, conceived as an essentially moral movement. But my limited experience of the Mahajan of Champaran has made me revise the accepted opinion about his 'blighting influence.' I have found him to be not always relentless, not always exacting of the last pie. He sometimes serves his clients in many ways or even comes to their rescue in the hour of their distress. My observation is so limited that I dare not draw any conclusions from it, but I respectfully enquire whether it is not possible to make a serious effort to draw out the good in the Mahajan and help him or induce him to throw out the evil in him. May he not be induced to join the army of co-operation, or has experience proved that he is past praying for?

I note that the movement takes note of all

indegenous industries. I beg publicly to express my gratitude to Government for helping me in my humble effort to improve the lot of the weaver. The experiment I am conducting shows that there is a vast field for work in this direction. No well wisher of India, no patriot dare look upon the impending destruction of the hand-loom weaver with equanimity. As Dr. Mann has stated, this industry used to supply the peasant with an additional source of livelihood and an insurance against famine. Every Registrar who will nurse back to life this important and graceful industry will earn the gratitude of India. My humble effort consists firstly in making researches as to the possibilities of simple reforms in the orthodox hand-looms, secondly in weaning the educated youth from the craving for Government or other service and the feeling that education renders him unfit for independent occupation and in inducing him to take to weaving as a calling as honourable as that of a barrister or a doctor, and thirdly by helping those weavers who have abandoned their occupation to revert to it. I will not weary the audience with any statement on the first two parts of the experiment. The third may be allowed a few sentences as it has a direct bearing upon the subject before us. I was able to enter upon it only six months ago. Five families that had left off the calling have reverted to it and they are doing a prosperous business. The Ashram supplies them at the door with the yarn they need; its volunteers take delivery of the cloth woven, paying them cash at the market rate. The Ashram merely loses interest on the loan advanced for the yarn. It has as yet suffered no loss and is able to restrict its loss to a minimum by limiting the loan to a particular figure. All future transactions are strictly cash. We are able to command a ready sale for the cloth received. The loss of interest, therefore, on the transaction is negligible. I would like the audience to note, its purely moral character from start to finish. The Ashram depends for its existence on such help as *friends* render it. We, therefore, can have no warrant for charging interest. The weavers could not be saddled with it. Whole families that were breaking to pieces are put together again. The use of the loan is predetermined. And we the middlemen being volunteers obtain the privilege of entering into the lives of these families, I hope for their and our betterment. We cannot lift them without being lifted ourselves. This last relationship has not yet been developed, but we hope at an early date to take in hand the education too of these families and not rest satisfied till we have touched them at every point. This is not too ambitious a dream. God willing, it will be a reality some day. I have ventured to dilate upon the small experiment to illustrate what I mean by co-operation to present it to others for imitation. Let us be sure of our ideal. We shall ever fail to realize it, but we should never cease to strive for it. Then there need be no fear of "co-operation of scoundrels" that Ruskin so rightly dreaded.

INDIAN COLONIAL EMIGRATION

I have carefully read the resolution issued at Simla by the Government of India on the 1st instant (September 1917) embodying the report of the Inter-Departmental Conference recently held in London. It will be remembered that this was the Conference referred to in the Viceregal speech of last year at the opening of the sessions of the Viceregal Legislative Council. It will be remembered, too, that this was the Conference which Sir James Meston and Sir S. P. Sinha were to have attended, but were unable to attend owing to their having returned to India before the date of the meeting of the Conference. It is stated in the report under discussion that these gentlemen were able to discuss the question of emigration to certain English Colonies informally with the two Secretaries of State, *i.e.*, the Secretary of State for India and the Secretary of State for the Colonies. Lord Islington, Sir A. Steel Maitland, and Messrs. Seton, Grindle, Green and Macnaughton constituted the Conference. To take the wording of the resolution, this

Conference sat "to consider the proposals for a new assisted system of emigration to British Guiana, Trinidad, Jamaica and Fiji." The public should, therefore, note that this assisted emigration is to be confined only to the four Crown Colonies mentioned and not to the Self-Governing Colonies of South Africa, Canada or Australia, or the Crown Colony of Mauritius. What follows will show the importance of this distinction. It is something to be thankful for that "the Government of India have not yet considered the report and reserved judgment on all the points raised in it." This is as it should be on a matter so serious as this and one which only last year fairly convulsed the whole of India and which as in one shape or another agitated the country since 1895.

The declaration too that "His Majesty's Government in agreement with the Government of India have decided that indentured emigration shall not be re-opened" is welcome as is also the one that "no free emigrants can be introduced into any Colony until all Indian emigrants already there have been released from existing indentures."

In spite, however, of so much in the report that fills one with gladness, the substantive part of it which sets forth the scheme which is to replace indentured emigration is, so far as one can judge, to say the least of it, disappointing. Stripped of all the phraseology under which the scheme has been veiled, it is nothing less than a system of indentured emigration no doubt on a more humane basis and safeguarded with some conditions beneficial to the emigrants taking advantage of it.

The main point that should be borne in mind is that the Conference sat designedly to consider a scheme of emigration not in the interests of the Indian labourer, but in those of the colonial employer. The new system, therefore, is devised to help the Colonies concerned. India needs no outlet, at any rate for the present moment, for emigration outside the country. It is debateable whether in any event the four Colonies will be the most suitable for Indian Colonisation. The best thing, therefore, that can happen from an Indian standpoint is that there should be no assisted emigration from India of any type whatsoever. In the absence of any such assistance, emigration will have to be entirely free and at the risk and expense of the emigrant himself. Past experience shows that in that event there will be very little voluntary emigration to distant Colonies. In the report, assisted emigration means, to use a mild expression, stimulated emigration; and surely with the industries of India crying out for labour and with her legitimate resources yet undeveloped, it is madness to think of providing a stimulus for the stay-at-home Indian to go out of India. Neither the Government nor any voluntary agency has been found capable of protecting from ill usage the Indian who emigrates either to Burma or Ceylon, much less can any such protection avail in far off Fiji or the three other Colonies. I hope that leaders of public opinion in India will, therefore, take their stand on the one impregnable rock of not wanting any emigration whatsoever to the Colonies. It might be argued that we, as a component part of the Empire, are bound to consider the wants of our partners, but this would not be a fair plea to advance so long as India stands in need of all the labour she can produce, if, therefore India does not assist the Colonies, it is not because of want of will, but it is due to want of ability. An additional reason a politician would be justified in using is that, so long as India does not in reality occupy the position of an equal partner with the Colonies and so long as her sons continue to be regarded by Englishmen in the Colonies and English employers even nearer home to be fit only as hewers of wood and drawers of water, no scheme of emigration to the Colonies can be morally advantageous to Indian emigrants. If the badge of inferiority is always to be worn by them, they can never rise to their full status, and any material advantage they will gain by emigrating can, therefore, be of no consideration.

But let us for the moment consider the new system. "The system," it is stated, to be followed in future will be one of aided emigration, and its object will be to encourage the settlement of Indians in certain Colonies after a probationary period of employment in those Colonies, to train and fit them for life and work there and at the same time to acquire a supply of the labour essential to the well-being of the colonists themselves." So the re-settlement is to be conditional on previous employment under contract, and it will be seen in the course of our examination that this contract is to be just as binding as the contracts used to be under indenture. The report has the following humorous passage in it: "He will be in no way restricted to service under any particular employer except that for his own protection, a selected employer will be chosen for him for the first six months." This has a flavour of the old indentured system. One of the evils complained of about that system was that the labourer was assigned to an employer. He was not free to choose one himself. Under the new system, the employer is to be selected for the protection of the labourer. It is hardly necessary for me to point out that the would be labourer will never be able to feel the protection devised for him. The labourer is further "to be encouraged to work for his first three years in agricultural industries, by the offer, should he do so, of numerous and important benefits subsequently as a colonist." This is another inducement to indenture, and I know enough of such schemes to be able to assure both the Government and public that these so-called inducements in the hands of clever manipulations become nothing short of methods of compulsion in respect of innocent and ignorant Indian labourers. It is due to the framers of the scheme that I should draw attention to the fact that they have avoided all criminal penalties for breach of contract. In India, itself, if the scheme is adopted, we are promised a revival of the much dreaded depots and Emigration Agents, all no doubt on a more respectable basis, but still of the same type and capable of untold mischief.

The rest of the report is not likely to interest the public but those who wish to study it will, I doubt not, come to the conclusion to which I have been driven, that the framers have done their best to strip the old system of many of the abuses which had crept into it, but they have not succeeded in placing before the Indian public an acceptable scheme. I hold that it was an impossible task. The system of indenture was one of temporary slavery; it was incapable of being amended; it should only be ended and it is to be hoped that India will never consent to its revival in any shape or form.—(*Indian Review*).

INDIAN RAILWAYS

I have now been in India far over two years and a half after my return from South Africa. Over one quarter of that time I have passed on the Indian trains travelling 3rd class by choice. I have travelled up north as far as Lahore, down South up to Tranquebar, and from Karachi to Calcutta. Having resorted to 3rd class travelling among other reasons for the purpose of studying the conditions under which this class of passengers travel, I have naturally made as critical observations as I could. I have fairly covered the majority of railway systems during this period. Now and then I have entered into correspondence with the management of the different Railways about the defects that have come under my notice. But I think that the time has come when I should invite the Press and the Public to join in a crusade against a grievance which has too long remained unredressed though much of it is capable of redress without great difficulty.

On the 12th instant (September 1917) I booked at Bombay for Madras by the Mail train and paid Rs. 13-9-0. It was labelled to carry 22 passengers. These could only have seating accommodation. There were no bunks in this carriage whereon passengers could lie with any degree of safety or comfort. There were two nights to be passed in this train before reaching Madras. If not more than 22 passengers found their way into my carriage before we reached Poona, it was because the bolder ones kept the others at bay. With the exception of two or three insistent passengers all had to find their sleep being seated all the time. After reaching Raichur the pressure became unbearable. The rush of passengers could not be stayed. The fighters among us found the task almost beyond them. The guards or other railway servants came in only to push in more passengers. A defiant Menon merchant protested against this packing of passengers like sardines. In vain did he say that this was his fifth night on the train. The guard insulted him and referred him to the management at the Terminus. There were during this time as many as 35 passengers in the carriage during the greater part of it. Some lay on the floor in the midst of dirt and some had to keep standing. A free fight was at one time avoided only by the intervention of some of the older passengers who did not want to add to the discomfort by an exhibition of temper.

On the way, passengers got down for tea tanni-water with filthy sugar and a whitish looking liquid miscalled milk which gave this water a muddy appearance. I can vouch for the appearance but I cite the testimony of the passengers as to the taste.

Not during the whole of the journey was the compartment once swept or cleaned. The result was that every time you walked on the floor or rather cut your way through the passengers seated on the floor, you waded through dirt.

The closet was also not cleaned during the journey and there was no water in the water tank.

Refreshments sold to the passengers were dirty looking, handled by dirtier hands, coming out of filthy receptacles and weighed in equally unattractive scales. These were previously sampled by millions of flies. I asked some of the passengers who went in for these dainties to give their opinion. Many of them used choice expressions as to the quality but were satisfied to state they were helpless in the matter; they had to take things as they came.

On reaching the station I found that the ghari-wala would not take me unless I paid the fare he wanted. I mildly protested and told him I would pay him the authorised fare. I had to turn a passive resister before I could be taken. I simply told him he would have to pull me out or call the policeman.

The return journey was performed in better manner. The carriage was packed already and but for a friend's intervention I would not have been able to secure even a seat. My admission was certainly beyond the authorised number. This compartment was constructed to carry 9 passengers but it had constantly 12 in it. At one place an impertinent railway servant swore at a protestant, threatened to strike him and locked the door over the passenger whom he had with difficulty squeezed in. To this compartment there was a closet falsely so-called. It was designed as a European closet but could hardly be used as such. There was a pipe in it but no water and I say without fear of challenge that it was pestilentially dirty.

The compartment itself was evil looking. Dirt was lying thick upon the wood work and I do not know that it had ever seen soap or water.

This compartment had an exceptional assortment of passengers. There were three stalwart Punjabi Mohammedans, two refined Tamilians and two Mohammedan merchants who joined us later. The merchant related the bribes they had to give to procure comfort. One of the Punjabis had already travelled three nights and was weary and fatigued. But he could not stretch himself. He said he had sat the whole day at the Central Station watching passengers giving bribes to procure their tickets. Another said he had himself to pay Rs. 5 before he could get his ticket and his seat. These three men were bound for Ludhiana and had still more nights of travel in store for them.

What I have described is not exceptional but normal. I have got down at Raichur, Dhond, Sonepur, Chakradharpur, Purulis, Asansol and other junction stations and been at the Mosafirkhanas attached to these stations.

They are discreditable-looking places where there is no order, no cleanliness but utter confusion and horrible din and noise. Passengers have no benches or not enough to sit on. They squat on dirty floors and eat dirty food. They are permitted to throw the leavings of their food and spit where they like, sit how they like and smoke every where. The closets attached to these places defy description. I have not the power to adequately describe them without committing a breach of the laws of decent speech. Disinfecting powder, ashes or disinfecting fluid are unknown. The army of flies buzzing about them warns you against their use. But a 3rd class traveller is dumb and helpless. He does not want to complain even though to go to these places, may be to court death. I know passengers who fast while they are travelling just in order to lessen the misery of their life in the trains. At Sonepur flies having failed, wasps have come forth to warn the public and the authorities but yet to no purpose. At the Imperial Capital a certain 3rd class booking office is a Black Hole fit only to be destroyed.

Is it any wonder that plague has become epedemic in India? Any other result is impossible where passengers always leave some dirt where they go and take more on leaving?

On Indian trains alone passengers smoke with impunity in all carriages irrespective of the presence of the fair sex and irrespective of the protests of nonsmokers and notwithstanding a byelaw which prevents a passenger from smoking without the permission of his fellow passengers in a compartment which is not allotted to smokers.

The existence of the awful war cannot be allowed to stand in the way of removal of this gigantic evil. War can be no warrant for tolerating dirt and overcrowding. One could understand an entire stoppage of passenger traffic in a crisis like this but never a continuation or accentuation of insanitation and conditions that must undermine health and morality.

Compare the lot of the 1st class passengers with that of the 3rd class. In the Madras case the 1st class fare is over five times as much as the 3rd class fare. Does the 3rd class passenger get one fifth, even one tenth, of the comfort of his 1st class fellow? It is but simple justice to claim that relative proportions be observed between the cost and the comfort.

It is a known fact that the 3rd class traffic pays for the ever-increasing luxuries of 1st and 2nd class travelling. Surely a 3rd class passenger is entitled at least to the bare necessities of life.

In neglecting the 3rd class passengers an opportunity of giving a splendid education to millions in orderliness, sanitation, decent composite life, and cultivation of simple and clean tastes is being lost. Instead of receiving an object lesson in these matters 3rd class passengers have their sense of decency and cleanliness blunted during their travelling experience.

Among the many suggestions that can be made for dealing with the evil here described I would respectfully include this : let the people in high places, the Viceroy, the Commander-in-Chief, the Rajahs, the Maharajas, the Imperial Councillors and others who generally travel in superior classes, without previous warning go through the experience now and then of 3rd class travelling. We would then soon see a remarkable change in the conditions of the 3rd class travelling and the uncomplaining millions will get some return for the fares they pay under the expectation of being carried from place to place with the ordinary creature comforts.

GUJARAT EDUCATIONAL CONFERENCE

[*The second Gujarat Educational Conference was held at Broach, in October* 20, 1917, *when Mr. M. K. Gandhi read his presidential address in Gujarati a translation of which reads as under*] :—

After thanking the conference for the honour bestowed on him he said the selection fell on him simply because he would yield to none in his love and devotion for the Gujarati language. He then congratulated the last conference on the good work done by them and for publishing a very valuable report in time. He then highly regretted the premature loss of Mr. Ranjitram Vavabhai, one of the most active secretaries of the conference. Recapitulating the three objects of the Gujarat Kalavani Mandal under whose auspices the conference was held, he proceeded to treat them in detail.

MEDIUM OF INSTRUCTION

He regarded the question of the medium of instruction of the highest importance and as one on which the whole edifice of education rested. He referred to the two views held on this question. There is one party that wants the mother tongue Gujarati to be the medium. The other party supports English. 'Both are prompted by pure motives. Both have the good of the country at heart but purity of motives alone is not sufficient for the achievement of the desired end. Experience of the world shows that often a pure motive lands us on impure ground. Let us therefore examine the merits or otherwise of the two views and see if we can arrive at unanimity on this point. This difficult question concerns the whole of India. But that does not mean that each province cannot solve it for itself, but must wait for general unanimity.'

Of course, it would help us to some degree in the solution of this problem if we review the agitation and efforts of other provinces. Bengal during the excitement of the 'partition' days tried to impart instruction in Bengali. Schools were established, funds poured in but the experiment failed. In my humble opinion it failed, because the organisers and teachers had not sufficient faith in their own experiment. The educated Bengali could not get out of the fascination of the English language. It was suggested that Bengali literature owes its development to the command the Bengalis have over the English language. In answer Mr. Gandhi instanced the wonderful Bengali of Sir Rabindranath Tagore which is in no way indebted to his knowledge of English. He owes inspiration to the very atmosphere of India. He has imbibed it from the Upanishads. The same can be said of Mahatma Munshi Ram and Pandit Madan Mohan Malaviya. The service which Swami Dayanand Sarasvati rendered to Hindi literature owed nothing to English. Tukaram and Ramdas who have enriched the Marathi language were not in the least under the obligation of the English language. English cannot claim any credit for the contribution to Gujarati literature of poets from Parmanand and Samel Bhat down to Dalpatram. When we consider how languages grow, we come to the conclusion that a language is but the reflection of the character of the people that speak it. Language depends upon the peculiar genius and occupation of a people. The inordinate use of polished and courtly forms of speech indicate that we have been under subjection for generations together. The English language abounds in nautical terms. We cannot import them in the Gujarati language, but if we take to navigation nautical phraseology will frame of itself.

Mr. Gandhi then proceeded to give a quotation from Rev. Taylor's grammar of the Gujarati language in support of the above.

He then referred to the laudable efforts of the Arya Samaj in making Hindi the medium of instruction in their *Gurukul*; and of the Telugu people in using Telugu as the vehicle of education. In Maharastra Professor Karve and Prof. Naick both work in the same direction. In Professor Bijapurkar's school they had already prepared suitable text-books in Marathi. They are all hopeful about the success of their work. In Gujarat there was a movement already for imparting instruction through Gujarati. Prof. Gajjar and the late Dewan Bahadur Manibhai Jarbhai may be regarded as the pioneers and it now remains with us to consider whether we shall water the plant sown by them or allow it to wither away.

Experienced teachers say that what takes sixteen years to learn through English can perfectly be acquired in ten years at the most through the vernaculars. If thousands of our students save six years each of their precious life, what a great national saving it would be.

The excessive burden of having to learn through a foreign medium has sapped the strength, enthusiasm and vitality of our young men. Sickly and pale they can at best be mere imitators. All power of initiative, originality and enterprise ; courage, discrimination and fearlessness dwindle away as years pass by. What they commence they cannot carry out. The few that show some spirit die young. The negroes of South Africa are a stalwart and sober race. Social evils like child-marriage are unknown amongst them but they too have suffered like ourselves because they accepted Dutch as the medium of their education. They have grown impotent imitators of the west. With the loss of their mother tongue they lost all vigour and originality. We who have received English education cannot measure the loss we have sustained. If we consider what little hold we have upon our masses we can have some idea of that loss. We are proud of a Bose or a Ray amongst us but I daresay that had we received instruction through the vernacular for the last fifty years we would have had amongst us so many Boses and Rays that their existence would not have been a matter of surprise to us.

Leaving aside the question whether Japan's activities are in the right direction or not we can say that the extraordinary enterprise and progressive life they have shown is due to their education being given in Japanese. Their education has infused a new life among the people which has been a wonder to the gaping world. Instruction through a foreign medium brings about untold evils.

There must be a correspondence between the impressions and expressions we receive with our mother's milk and the education we receive at school. A foreign medium destroys the correspondence, and whosoever helps this destruction, however pure his motives, is an enemy of his country. The evil does not stop here. The foreign medium has created an unnatural gulf between the educated classes and the masses at large. We do not understand the masses and the masses do not understand us. They regard us as foreigners and they fear and distrust us. If this state of things continues for long, Lord Curzon's charge that we do not represent the masses will some day prove to be true. Fortunately the educated classes have gradually come to realise the difficulty of reaching the masses. They see now that they have over reached the expectations of Lord Macaulay. We took to English because it led to the acquisition of wealth, and some cultivated the ideas of nationalism through English.

If we were in power we could see the danger of the spread of English at the cost of the vernacular. Even the Government officers have not dispensed with the vernaculars. In offices and law courts they still use the vernaculars. If pleaders conducted their cases in the vernaculars, the clients would gain a great deal, and the language would be enriched.

It is argued that only the English knowing Indians have evinced patriotism. Recent events prove otherwise, but even accepting the assertion we can say that others had no opportunity whatsoever. The patriotism of the English educated has not spread amongst the masses. English may be kept as an optional subject for those who want to study it for political purposes or for the acquisition of wealth by the help of western sciences. Not only should they acquire a good command over the English language but it is also our duty to make facilities for imparting such education.

Before closing this topic he referred to the two pamphlets published by Dr. P. J. Mehta and recommended the audience to peruse them. He then suggested a number of ways and means for preparing a ground for making Gujarati as the medium of instruction such as the use of Gujarati language only in mutual intercourse among the Gujaratis, preparation of Gujarati text-books, opening schools, etc.

NATIONAL LANGUAGE

After dealing with the medium of instruction he dwelt at length upon the subject of National language. He gave an able reply to those who suggest that English ought to become the *lingua franca* of India. He said a National language should satisfy the following five conditions:—

(1) It must be easy for the official.

(2) It must be the vehicle of religious, social and political intercourse of the people.

(3) It must be spoken by a large number.

(4) It must be easy of acquisition by the masses.

(5) It must not be considered a temporary makeshift arrangement.

He then showed how English does not satisfy any of these conditions. He proved that Hindi is the only language that satisfies all these conditions. Hindi was our national language even under the Mahomedan rule and the Mahomedan rulers did not think it proper to substitute it with Persian or Arabic.

He then pointed out the defects in the method of teaching history, geography, science and mathematics. He then also referred to the non-provision of such subjects as music, agriculture, military training, weaving, religion and hygiene.

ADVICE TO THE MERCHANTS

[*In reply to the address given to him by the merchants of Broach, Mr. Gandhi said*] :—

Merchants always have the spirit of adventure, intellect and wealth, as without these qualities their business cannot go on. But now they must have the fervour of patriotism in them. Patriotism is necessary even for religion. If the spirit of patriotism is awakened through the religious fervour, then that patriotism will shine out brilliantly. So it is necessary that patriotism must be roused in the mercantile community.

The merchants take more part in public affairs now-a-days than before. When merchants take to politics through patriotism, Swaraj is as good as obtained. Some of you might be wondering how we can get Swaraj. I lay my hand on my heart and say that, when the merchant class understands the spirit of patriotism, then only can we get Swaraj quickly. Swaraj then will be quite a natural thing.

Amongst the various keys which will unlock Swaraj to us, the Swadeshi Vow is the golden one. It is in the hands of the merchants to compel the observance of the Swadeshi Vow in the country, and this is an adventure which can be popularised by the merchants. I humbly request you to undertake this adventure, and then you will see what wonders you can do.

This being so, I have to say with regret that it is the merchant class which has brought ruin to the Swadeshi practice, and the Swadeshi movement in this country. Complaints have lately risen in Bengal about the increase of rates, and one of them is against Gujarat. It is complained there that the prices of Dhotis have been abnormally increased and Dhotis go from Gujarat. No one wants you not to earn money, but it must be earned righteously and not be ill-gotten. Merchants must earn money by fair means. Unfair means must never be used.

Continuing, Mr. Gandhi said: India's strength lies with the merchant class. So much does not lie even with the army. Trade is the cause of war, and the merchant class has the key of war in their hands. Merchants raise the money and the army is raised on the strength of it. The power of England and Germany rests on their trading class. A country's prosperity depends upon its mercantile community. I consider it as a sign of good luck that I should receive an address from the merchant class. Whenever I remember Broach, I will enquire if the merchants who have given me an address this day have righteous faith and patriotism. If I receive a disappointing reply, I will think that merely a wave of giving addresses had come over India and that I had a share in it.

VERNACULARS AS A MEDIA OF INSTRUCTION

It is to be hoped that Dr. Mehta's labour of love will receive the serious attention of English-Educated India. The following pages were written by him for the *Vedanta Kesari* of Madras and are now printed in their present form for circulation throughout India. The question of vernaculars as media of instruction is of national importance; neglect of the vernaculars means national suicide. One hears many protagonists of the English language being continued as the medium of instruction pointing to the fact that English educated Indians are the sole custodians of public and patriotic work. It would be monstrous if it were not so. For, the only education given in this country is through the English language. The fact, however, is that the results are not at all proportionate to the time we give to our education. We have not reacted on the masses. But I must not anticipate Dr. Mehta. He is in earnest. He writes feelingly. He has examined the *pros* and *cons* and collected a mass of evidence in support of his arguments. The latest pronouncement on the subject is that of the Viceroy. Whilst His Excellency is unable to offer a solution, he is keenly alive to the necessity of imparting instruction in our schools through the vernaculars. The Jews of middle and Eastern Europe, who are scattered in all parts of the world, finding it necessary to have a common tongue for mutual intercourse, have raised Yiddish to the status of a language, and have succeeded in translating into Yiddish the best books to be found in the world's literature. Even they could not satisfy the soul's yearning through the many foreign tongues of which they are masters; nor did the learned few among them wish to tax the masses of the Jewish population with having to learn a foreign language before they could realise their dignity. So they have enriched what was at one time looked upon as a mere jargon—but what the Jewish children learnt from their mothers—by taking special pains to translate into it the best thought of the world. This is a truly marvellous work. It has been done during the present generation, and Webster's

Dictionary defines it as a polyglot jargon used for inter-communication by Jews from different nations.

But a Jew of middle and Eastern Europe would feel insulted if his mother-tongue were now so described. If these Jewish scholars have succeeded, within a generation, in giving their masses a language of which they may feel proud, surely it should be an easy task for as to supply the needs of our own vernaculars, which are cultured languages. South Africa teaches us the same lesson. There was a duel there between the Taal, a corrupt form of Dutch, and English. The Boer mothers and the Boer fathers were determined that they would not let their children, with whom they in their infancy talked in the Taal, be weighed down with having to receive instruction through English. The case for English here was a strong one. It had able pleaders for it. But English had to yield before Boer patriotism. It may be observed that they rejected even the high Dutch. The school masters, therefore, who are accustomed to speak the polished Dutch of Europe, are compelled to teach the easier Taal. And literature of an excellent character is at the present moment growing up in South Africa in the Taal, which was only a few years ago, the common medium of speech between simple but brave rustics. If we have lost faith in our vernaculars, it is a sign of want of faith in ourselves; it is the surest sign of decay. And no scheme of self-Government however benevolently or generously it may be bestowed upon us, will ever make us a self-governing nation, if we have no respect for the languages our mothers speak.—(*Introduction contributed to Dr. P. J. Mehta's Pamphlet, No, 1*).

APPENDIX I

THE STRUGGLE OF PASSIVE RESISTANCE MOVEMENT IN SOUTH AFRICA

(By the Editor, Indian Opinion.)

To survey, within a limited space, the origins and incidents of a movement that has occupied eight years of the history of South African Indians is a task impossible of satisfactory fulfilment. The present sketch will, therefore, be but a hasty outline, with here and there an indicator emphasising a noteworthy occurrence or a fundamental outline.

The origins of the Passive Resistance Struggle are to be sought, not in the agitation of 1906, but in that which commenced, in one of its phases, in the Transvaal. In 1885, and, in another, in Natal, in 1894. The old Republican Law 3 of 1885, whilst imposing various burdens upon Asiatics residing in the country, required that such of them as entered for purposes of trade should be registered at a fixed fee, and that, "for sanitary purposes," they should reside in locations specially set apart for them. To a large extent, both requirements proved a dead letter, but a great deal of friction with the British Government was engendered, resulting in Imperial intervention at the time of the War, when resident Indians, as British subjects, were promised complete redress of their grievances.

In Natal, a British Colony, the position had been complicated by the grave prejudice aroused by the presence of large numbers of Indian labourers brought at the instance of the European Colonists under indenture, and an agitation had arisen for the exclusion of free Asiatic immigration and the disfranchisement of all Asiatics. It became a question whether this was to be accomplished by specifically racial legislation or by general enactment differentially administered. The conflict of views represented by these two methods raged for sometime, but at last, thanks to the statesmanship of Mr. Chamberlain, in 1897, the second method was adopted, and the famous "Natal Act" passed, imposing an educational and not a racial test. From then onwards, in Natal, racial legislation was a thing of the past, and hence the first signs of renewed trouble arose in the Transvaal, where the principle of statutory equality had not been accepted, owing to a different political conception of the status of coloured people.

In the re-settlement that took place after the War, it was hoped that the burdens would be removed.

from the shoulders of the British Indian community but Indians were dismayed to find the Imperial authorities endeavouring vigorously to enforce the obnoxious legislation against which they had strongly protested in pre-war days, a policy that was later weakly defended by Lord Selborne. Immigration of Indians was severely restricted by the Peace Preservation Ordinance. Re-registration of practically all adult male Indians, under Law 3 of 1885, was urged by Lord Milner, and was subsequently agreed to by the Indian leaders as a purely voluntary act, on Lord Milner's definite promise that this registration would be regarded as complete and final, and that the certificates issued would constitute a permanent right of residence to the holders and a right to come and go at will.

Meanwhile, Law 3 of 1885 was being enforced so as to compel all Indians to reside and trade in locations, and the pre-war controversy was revived, resulting in an appeal to the Supreme Court, which reversed the old Republican High Court's decision, and held that Indians were free to trade anywhere they pleased, and that non-residence in a location was not punishable at law. This decision was a severe rebuff to the anti-Indian element in the European population that had its representatives even in the Government, which endeavoured to legislate to overcome the effect of the Supreme Court decision—without result, however, owing to the intervention of the then Secretary of State for the Colonies, the late Mr. Lyttelton. But the general public, by ingeniously manipulated statistics, were led to believe in a huge influx of unauthorised Asiatics into the Transvaal, to which some colour was let by the dispersal of the Indian residents of the Johannesburg Indian location throughout the Colony, after it was burnt down at the time of the plague outbreak in 1904, and meetings all over the Transvaal were held with the object of closing the door against all Asiatic immigration, and compelling Indians to trade and reside exclusively in locations. In an atmosphere of prejudice and terror thus created, it was possible effectively to protest one's innocence, and the request of the Indian community for an open and impartial inquiry, whether by Royal Commission or otherwise, fell on deaf ears; so that when a draft ordinance was published, in 1906, to "amend" Law 3 of 1885, requiring compulsory re-registration of the entire Indian community, men, women, and children, it was voiciferously welcomed by the whole European population, whilst it fell amongst the Indian victims to be like a bomb-shell. The basic assumption, on the part of the authorities, for its necessity lay in the unquenchable belief in wholesale Indian immigration of an unlawful character, to which, in their opinion, resident Indians could not but be a party. So far as the general public was concerned, the measure was hailed as the first instalment of a scheme designed to drive Indians out of the Colony altogether, and Europeans in the neighbouring Colonies and territories eagerly looked on, as they had looked on, in 1903, at Lord Milner's abortive effort to compel Indian trade and residence in locations, so that they might take advantage of the results of the new policy to relieve themselves to their own Asiatic " incubus."

Appalled by the magnitude of the disaster that threatened the community, the Indian leaders hastened to take steps to avoid it, if possible. They sought an interview with the responsible member of the Government, but succeeded only in getting women excluded from the operation of the measure, and, as a last resort, an Indian mass meeting was held at the moment that the Legislative Council was debating the clauses of the draft ordinance. Whilst the Council's debate was a perfunctory and prearranged performance, the whole business being concluded in less than a couple of hours, the crowded Empire Theatre rang with impassioned denunciations of the Government's policy, which belied the solemn undertaking of Lord Milner in every important respect, assumed the guilt of the Indian community unheard and without proof, and adumbrated their virtual expulsion from the Colony, and, eventually, from South Africa. So fierce was the indignation aroused that, when the famous Fourth Resolution was put, committing all present, and those they represented, to go to gaol, if the measure should become law, until such time as it should be repealed or disallowed, the whole vast audience of three thousand persons rose as one man, and shouted a solemn "Amen," when the oath of Passive Resistance was administered. Simultaneously, however, and as a last effort to avoid a terrible conflict, a deputation to England was arranged for. The delegates proceeded there to interview the Imperial authorities and arouse public opinion, and their efforts resulted in the suspension of the Royal Assent to the measure owing to the imminence of the inauguration of self-government in the Transvaal, and in the formation of the famous South Africa British Indian Committee, with Sir Mancherji Bhownaggree as its Executive Chairman, Mr. L. W. Ritch as its Secretary, and, subsequently, Lord Ampthill as its President.

The disallowance of the measure was, however, merely a temporary respite, for, taking umbrage at what was thought to be an impertinent intrusion on the part of the Imperial Government in the affairs of a practically self-governing British Colony, the European section of the population angrily demanded the immediate re-enactment of the ordinance, and almost the first action of the new Parliament was to

SIR M. M. BHOWNAGGREE,
Chairman South Africa British Indian Committee, London.

MR. RATAN TATA,
A Patriotic Indian donor of munificent contributions to the Passive Resistence Fund.

rush it through all its stages in a single session of a unanimous House, entirely ignoring Indian opinion and Indian protests, for, as Indians were not directly represented in Parliament, nobody appeared to consider it necessary to take their feelings into consideration.

Still anxious to avoid a struggle that had appeared to be inevitable, the Indian leaders had urged the Government and Parliament not to proceed with the Bill, but to accept a voluntary effort of re-registration in a manner that might be mutually agreed upon, in which they proffered all possible assistance. But they were distrusted and ignored, and all the tragic possibilities of a prolonged conflict were forced upon the Indian community. In July, 1907, the new Act came into force, and registration under it officially commenced, in compartments, the registration officers travelling from town to town throughout the Colony. Their efforts to induce registration were wholly unsuccessful, and an extension of the advertised time for registration was given by the Government, as a last opportunity to comply with the law. But 95 per cent. of the Indian community remained true to its oath. Meanwhile, a further effort had been made to avoid an extension of the trouble, and a petition, signed by some 3,000 Indians, had been addressed to the Government, imploring them to realise the depth of suffering into which it was threatened to plunge the Indian community, who once more offered voluntary re-registration if the Act was suspended. The petition was rejected contemptuously, and, at the end of the year, several of the leaders were arrested, ordered to leave the Colony, and, upon their refusal to do so, imprisoned for various periods. This process was repeated, until some hundreds of all classes were lodged in gaol, and the Government, realising that their efforts to crush the community had failed, opened up negotiations through the agency of Mr. Albert Cartwright, then Editor of the *Transvaal Leader*, with the result that, almost at the moment that H. H. the Aga Khan was presiding over a huge public meeting of protest in Bombay, a compromise was signed, whereby it was agreed to suspend passive resistance, to proceed with voluntary re-registration for a period of three months, during which the operation of the law was to be suspended, and, as the Indian signatories clearly understood, to repeal the hated Act if the re-registration was satisfactorily completed. In the meantime, the situation had been complicated by the passing of an Immigration Act that, operating jointly with the Asiatic Law Amendment Act, absolutely prohibited all Asiatic immigration, no matter how cultured the immigrant might be. Thus, at a stroke, the policy of non-racial legislation, that had been so strongly advocated by Mr. Chamberlain, was destroyed. The community, however, realised that, with the repeal of the Asiatic Act, the racial taint would disappear and all efforts were, accordingly, concentrated upon that. The commencement of voluntary re-registration was signalised by a murderous attack upon Mr. Gandhi by a misguided countryman, and, for the moment, everything was in confusion. But a special appeal to the community was made, and, with confidence restored and the promise of repeal, re-registration was duly completed by the middle of May, and Lord Selborne himself bore testimony to its satisfactoriness. Then the Government were called upon to perform their part of the compromise, but the promise of repeal was repudiated, and immediately the Indian community was thrown into a turmoil. The Government offered to repeal the Act provided that certain classes of Indians were treated as prohibited immigrants, and the racial bar remained in the Immigration Law. Naturally, these terms were indignantly rejected, and the community prepared for a revival of Passive Resistance. Mr. Sorabji Shapurji, an educated Parsee from Natal, was imprisoned as a protest against the racial bar. The Natal Indian leaders entered the Transvaal, in order to co-operate with their brethren there, and were arrested as prohibited immigrants and ordered to leave the

Colony. But at a mass meeting held in Johannesburg, at which they were present, hundreds of certificates of voluntary registration were publicly burnt, and a challenge of wholesale imprisonment was thrown out to the Government, who took alarm at the situation, and a Conference of leading members of the Government and Opposition, and of representatives of the Indian and Chinese communities, together with Mr. Albert Cartwright, as mediator, was held at Pretoria. The Conference proved abortive, however, for, though they were prepared to waive the other points upon which they had previously insisted, the Government proved adamant on the two main issues. They definitely refused either to repeal the Asiatic Act or to remove the racial bar of the Immigration Law. An amending Bill was passed through both Houses of Parliament, validating voluntary registration, and improving the Indian position in certain respects, but it being, in the main, unsatisfactory for the reasons given above, it was not recognised by the Passive Resisters, who resumed the struggle with energy. The new measure, however, strengthened the hands of the Government by giving them powers of deportation, which, however, were at first neutralised by their deporting Passive Resisters across the Natal border, whence they returned as fast as they were deported.

LORD AMPTHILL,

President of the South Africa British Indian Committee, **London.**

Into the many details and ramifications of the struggle at this stage it is unnecessary now to enter; suffice it to recall the Delagoa Bay incidents, when the Portuguese Government acted as the catspaw of the Transvaal, in preventing the entry into the Transvaal of returning Indians lawfully resident there, the various test-cases brought in the Supreme Court against the Government, some of which were lost and some won, the voluntary insolvency of Mr. A. M. Cachalia, the Chairman of the British Indian Association, who preferred to keep his oath and preserve his honour to the sordid joy of money-making, the imprisonment of Indians of all classes by hundreds, the appeals to India, where protest meetings were held in different parts of the country, the financial help of Natal, the arousing of enthusiasm amongst Indians all over the country, the activity of Lord Ampthill's Committee in London, and of the British Press, the bitter controversies that raged in the Transvaal papers, the latent sympathy of not a few Transvaal Europeans culminating in the formation of Mr. Hosken's Committee, that rendered such splendid and patriotic service in a number of ways, the public letter to the *Times*, the refusal of the Royal Assent to anti-Indian measures passed by the Legislatures of Natal and Southern Rhodesia, the Indian mass meetings in Johannesburg and all over South Africa, the weakening of some sections of the Indian community and the strengthening of others, the amazing revelation of Tamil strength and fortitude, the energetic labours of the Indian women, the ruin and desolation of business and homes, the cruel jail hardships whose purpose was to crush the spirit of the Passive Resisters, the magnificent courage of those who sought imprisonment again and again, the glorious religious spirit that was developed as the struggle moved on from phase to phase, to hopes and fears, the firm faith of the leaders in ultimate success —all these constitute a pageant of incidents and emotions that gave greatness to the Passive Resistance movement, and that bestowed upon it its most distinguishing characteristics.

New life was given to the movement in the middle of 1909, when two deputations were authorised to proceed to England and India respectively, to cultivate public opinion there and to seek assistance. As the delegates were on the point of leaving, the majority of them were arrested and imprisoned as passive resisters, doubtless with the intention of preventing the departure of the remainder. But the community insisted that the deputations should go. In England, interest in the question was strongly revived, and, as Transvaal Ministers were there at the time in connection with the Draft Act of Union, the Imperial authorities strove to effect a settlement; but General Smuts proved obdurate, and flatly declined to remove the statutory racial bar and substitute for it general legislation, though it was clear that the Asiatic Act was doomed. The deputation, which had been led by Mr. Gandhi, therefore returned to South Africa, having accomplished only a part of what it had hoped to achieve, but having arranged for a body of volunteers who undertook to collect funds and keep the subject before the public.

The deputation to India, heralded by the tragic death of Nagappan shortly after his release from prison, was of a different character. Mr. Polak, who was the sole remaining delegate, placed himself unreservedly in the hands of the Hon. Mr. Gokhale, whose Servants of India Society arranged for meetings to be held in every part of the country, from Bombay to Rangoon, from Madras to Lahore. Tremendous enthusiasm was aroused, Indian patriotic pride in the sufferers in South Africa was awakened, and funds were energetically collected, following the example of Mr. Ratan J. Tata, some £10,000 being contributed for the maintenance of the struggle, ruling princes, sending generous subscriptions. All sections of the people united in demanding the intervention of the Imperial Government, and at the historic session of the Imperial Council at Calcutta, the Government of India announced its acceptance of Mr. Gokhale's resolution, unanimously supported, to take powers to prohibit the further recruitment of indentured labour in India for Natal. After a thirteen months' campaign, India had been educated on the South African Indian question to a degree that aroused the attention and anxiety of the Home authorities, and when angry protests came from every part of the country against the Transvaal Government's action in deporting to India large numbers of Passive Resisters (many of them born in South Africa), with the object of breaking up the movement, the Imperial Government, upon the urgent representations of the Government of India, successfully implored the Transvaal—and subsequently, the Union—Administration to cease to deport. The deportees subsequently returned to South Africa, but with the loss of Narayansamy, who died at Delagoa Bay after having been unlawfully denied a landing anywhere in British territory.

Meanwhile, the four South African Colonies had become Provinces of the Union of South Africa, and the Imperial Government, convinced at last of the justice of the Indian cause, and taking advantage of the possibilities of the new situation, addressed to the Union Government the memorable despatch of October 7, 1910, in which they powerfully recommended the repeal of Act 2 of 1907, the removal of the racial bar, and the substitution for the latter of the Indian suggestion of non-racial legislation modified by administrative differentiation, effectively limiting future Indian immigration to a minimum number annually of highly educated men, whose services would be required for the higher needs of the Indian community. To this despatch was appended the condition that nothing that was done to settle the Transvaal controversy at the expense of the Indians residing in the Coast Provinces would be satisfactory to the Imperial Government. The Union Ministers responded in a friendly manner, the struggle became less acute, and ultimately, in 1911, a Union Immigration Bill was published, purporting to settle the controversy that had been raging for so long. The new measure, however, obviously did not serve its purpose, for, whilst repealing the Asiatic Act of 1907, saving the rights of minors that had been declared by the Appellate Division of the Surpreme Court, in the Chotabhai case, the Bill did not remove the racial bar, but rather extended it throughout the Union, by reason of the Orange Free State entry question, and it took away other rights not only from Transvaal Indians, but from those resident in the Coast Provinces. An unanimous outcry arose from them, negotiations were re-opened, and the suggestion was thrown out by the Passive Resistance leaders that the Bill should be replaced by one limited to the Transvaal alone, which, however, was not adopted. Eventually it was found impossible to pass the Bill, and a provisional settlement was arranged, whereby the Indians undertook to suspend Passive Resistance, whilst the Government promised to introduce satisfactory legislation in the 1912 session of Parliament, meanwhile administering the law as though it had already been altered, and specially exempting, in terms of an earlier understanding, a limited number of educated entrants into the Transvaal.

Taking advantage of the lull, and of the better feeling aroused at the time of the King's Coronation in India, a further mission was sent there, in order to maintain public interest and to place before the Government the points upon which the Indian community insisted. The measure of 1912, however, met with no better fate than its predecessor, and the provisional agreement was extended for another year. It was then that preparations were made throughout South Africa to welcome the Hon. Mr. Gokhale, whose tour in the sub-continent is still fresh in the minds of all. He succeeded, as no one else had yet done in raising the discussion of the Indian problem to the Imperial plane, and won the admiration even of his opponents of his moderation and statesmanship. It was during this visit that Indians later alleged, on his authority, that a promise of repeal of the iniquitous £3 tax was made by the Government in view of the fact that, for over a year, further indentured immigration from India had been prohibited by the Indian Government.

When the 1913 Bill, however, was introduced into Parliament, and the Indian leaders observed the spirit in which the Indian question was dealt with by the Union Ministers, grave fears were aroused that a situation, which had already become still further complicated by the position created by the Searle judgment, invalidating practically every Indian marriage would once more developinto a catastrophe. The Government were warned that the marriage question must be settled if peace were desired, and that the racial bar must be finally removed from the measure. Amendments were introduced and accepted by the Government, purporting to settle the marriage controversy on the basis of the recognition of *de facto* monogamous marriages, but, even as passed, the Bill failed to satisfy the demands of the Passive Resisters, whilst the £3 tax remained unrepealed. A final attempt was made by the Indian leaders to avoid a revival of the struggle, and negotiations were once more opened with the Government, so as to obtain a promise of remedial legislation in the next session of Parliament. They were, however, interrupted by the European strike, during the heat of which Mr. Gandhi, as spokesman of the Passive Resisters, undertook to refrain from pressing the Indian case for the moment. Meanwhile, a mission had proceeded to England to co-operate with the Hon. Mr. Gokhale, at his urgent invitation, in order to bring home to the Imperial Government and the British public the extreme gravity of the situation, and the certainty of the extension of the demands of Passive Resisters unless a settlement of the points in dispute were promptly arrived at. All these representations, however, failed to conciliate the Union Government, which proved obdurate, and a final warning was sent to them stating that unless assurances of the introduction of legislative and administrative measures, in the following session, were given to recognise in law the validity of *de facto* monogamous marriage, to remove the racial bar, as regards the Free State, to restore the right of entry into the Cape Colony to South African-born Indians, to repeal the £3 tax, and to administer justly and with due regard to vested interests existing legislation operating harshly against Indians, Passive Resistance would be immediately revived. The warning was ignored, and the struggle was resumed in all its bitterness and on a much wider scale than before. Its incidents are too fresh in the public mind to need more than a brief mention—the compaign of the Indian women whose marriages had been dishonoured by a fresh decision of the Supreme Court, at the instigation of the Government, the awakening of the free and indentured labourers all over Natal, the tremendous strikes, the wonderful and historic strikers' march of protest into the Transvaal, the horrible scenes enacted into the latter in the effort to crush the strikers and compel them to resume work, the arrest and imprisonment of the principal leaders and of hundreds—almost thousands—of the rank and file, the enormous Indian mass meetings held in Durban, Johannesburg, and other parts of the Union, the fierce and passionate indignation aroused in India, the large sums of money poured into South Africa from all parts of the Motherland, Lord Hardinge's famous speech at Madras, in which he placed himself at the head of Indian public opinion and his demand for a Commission of Inquiry, the energetic efforts of Lord Ampthill's Committee, the hurried intervention of the Imperial authorities, the appointment over the heads of the Indian community of a Commission whose personnel could not satisfy the Indians, the discharge of the leaders whose advice to ignore the Commission was almost entirely accepted, the arrival of Messrs. Andrews and Pearson and their wonderful work of reconciliation, the deaths of Harbatsingh and Valiamma, the strained position relieved only by the interruption of the second European strike, when Mr. Gandhi once more undertook not to hamper the Government whilst they had their hands full with the fresh difficulty, and, when it had been dealt with, the entirely new spirit of friendliness, trust, and co-operation that was found to have been created by the moderation of the great Indian leader and the loving influence spread around him by Mr. Andrews as he proceeded with his great Imperial mission.

All these things are of recent history, as are the favourable recommendation of the Commission on practically every point referred to it and out of which Passive Resistance had arisen, the adoption of the commission's Report in its entirety by the Government, the introduction and passing into law of the Indians' Relief Act, after lengthy and remarkable debates in both Houses of the Legislature, the correspondence between Mr. Gandhi and General Smuts, in which the latter undertook, on behalf of the Government, to carry through the administrative reforms that were not covered by the new Act, and the Indian protagonist of passive Resistance formally announced the conclusion of the struggle and set forth the points upon which Indians would sooner or latter have to be satisfied before they could acquire complete equality of civil status—and the final scenes of departure, enacted throughout the country, wherein the deaths and sufferings of the Indian martyrs, Nagappen, Naryansamy, Harbatsingh, and Valiamma, were justified and sanctified to the world.

It is significant that, as Passive Resistance became stronger and purer, it succeeded more and more in bringing together the best representatives of the European and Indian sections of the population. With each new phase came new triumphs and new friends. Whilst every material gain has been put the restoration of that which was taken away, each gain of principle has been the concession of that which had been denied. The struggle commenced with a protest against the universal distrust and contempt for the Indian community. That distrust and contempt have been exchanged for trust and respect. It commenced with the complete ignoring of Indian sentiment. Gradually that policy, too, was altered, save that it revived acutely when the Commission was appointed over the heads of those mainly interested in its findings. To-day, however, the leaders are consulted in matters vitally affecting the welfare of the Indian community, and Passive Resistance has given for these disfranchised ones far more than the vote could have won, and in a shorter time. The movement commenced with a demand for the repeal of the Transvaal Act 2 of 1907. The Act was repealed and its threatened extension to other parts of South Africa was completely prevented. At the beginning, racial legislation against Indians was threatened, so as to drive them from the Colony.

The settlement has removed the possibility of racial legislation against Indians throughout the Empire. The system of indentured immigration from India, that had been regarded almost as a permanent feature of South African economics, has been ended. The hated £3 tax has been repealed and its attendant misery and insult destroyed. Vested rights, that were tending everywhere to disappear, are to be maintained and protected. The bulk of Indian marriages, that had never previously received the sanction of South African law, are henceforth to be fully recognised in law. But above and beyond all this is the new spirit of conciliation that has resulted from the hardships, the sufferings, the sacrifices of the Passive Resisters. The flag of legal racial equality has been kept flying, and it is now recognised that Indians have rights and aspirations and ideals that cannot be ignored. The struggle has more than proved the immense superiority of right over might, of soul-force over brute-force, of love and reason over hate and passion. India has been raised in the scale of nations, her children in South Africa have been ennobled, and the way is now open to them to develop their capacities in peace and concord, and thus contribute their quota to the building up of this great new nation that is arising in the South African sub-continent.

APPENDIX II

[*Mr. M. K. Gandhi in submitting an account of the Indian Committee of the income and expenditure up to the* 31*st January* 1915 *in connection with the Passive resistance in South Africa made the following observations*] :—

This struggle had defined principles and removed disabilities which were in the shape of a national insult. The larger qnestion of the treatment of British Indians who come from outside can be dealt with here. For the question of the local disabilities still unredressed, the Indian Committee will have to exercise a ceaseless watch and assist, as heretofore, the efforts of our countrymen in South Africa. I feel that I ought to place on record my strong conviction based upon the close personal observation extending over a period of twenty years that the system of indentured emigration is an evil which cannot be mended, but can only be ended. No matter how humane employers may be, it does not lend itself to the moral well-being of the men affected by it. I, therefore feel that your committee should lose no time in approaching the Government of India with a view to securing the entire abolition of the system for every part of the Empire. I am bound to mention that the struggle would not have ended so soon or even as satisfactorily as it did, but for the generous support rendered by the Motherland under the leadership of the great and saintly patriot, the late Mr. Gokhale, and but for the very sympathetic and firm attitude taken by the nobleman who at present occupies the Viceregal chair.

HISTORY OF PASSIVE RESISTANCE IN SOUTH AFRICA

Mr. Gandhi in the course of his letter to the Secretary, South African Committee, gives the following brief account of the struggle of passive resisters in South Africa, to the maintenance of which India contributed so generously.

"Whilst the actual courting of imprisonment has ceased, the struggle itself has by no means ended. In its last stages nearly 25,000 Indians actively participated in it, that is one sixth of the total Indian population in South Africa. The rest of the community practically with but few exceptions, supported the struggle either by contribution in cash or in kind or by holding meetings, etc. It began in Transvaal with the passing of the now famous Asiatic Registration Bill. In the year the struggle rolled on with temporary settlements. It included many other things besides the Asiatic Registration Act, and covered the whole of South Africa at the time of the settlement. The points in the passive resistance were as follows: (1) Repeal of the Asiatic Act. (2) Removal of racial or colour disqualification as to immigration from Union legislation. (3) Removal of legal disabilities of Indian wives (4) Removal of annual Poll Tax of £3 which was payable by ex-indentured Indians, their wives and grown-up children. (5) Just administration of the existing laws with due regard to vested rights.

All these points are covered by the settlement of the last year, which I consider to be a complete vindication of the passive resistance, and I venture to state that if more has not been gained more was not and could not be asked for as an item in the passive resistance, for a passive resister has to frame his minimum as well as his maximum, and he dare not ask for more nor can he be satisfied with less.

FUTURE WORK

But I do not wish to be understood to mean that nothing further remains to be done in South Africa, or that everything has been gained. We have only fought for the removal of legal disabilities as to immigration, but administratively we have taken note of the existing conditions and prejudices. We fought to keep the theory of the British Constitution in tact so that the practice may some day approach the theory as near as possible. There are still certain laws in South Africa, for instance, the law of 1885, the trade license laws of the Cape and Natal, which continue to cause worry. The administration of the Immigration Law is not all that it should be. For these, however, passive resistance is not applied and is at present inapplicable, its application being confined to grievances which are generally felt in a community and are known to hurt its self-respect or conscience. Any of the grievances referred to by me may, any day, advance to that stage. Till then, only the ordinary remedies of petition etc., can be adopted. Letters received from South Africa, show that difficulties are being experienced in some cases acutely by our countrymen, and if much has not been heard of them in India just now, it is because of the extraordinary self-restraint of our countrymen in South Africa, during the crisis that has overtaken the Empire.

AHIMSA

There seems to be no historical warrant for the belief that an exaggerated practice of Ahimsa synchronised with our becoming bereft of manly virtues! During the past 1,500 years we have, as a nation, given ample proof of physical courage, but we have been torn by internal dissensions and have been dominated by love of self instead of love of country.

We have, that is to say, been swayed by the spirit of irreligion rather than of religion.

I do not know how far the charge of unmanliness can be made good against the Jains. I hold no brief for them. By birth I am a Vaishnavite, and was taught Ahimsa in my childhood. I have derived much religious benefit from Jain religious works as I have from scriptures of the other great faiths of the world. I owe much to the living company of the deceased philosopher, Rajachand Kavi, who was a Jain by birth. Thus, though my views on Ahimsa are a result of my study of most of the faiths of the world, they are now no longer dependent upon the authority of these works. They are a part of my life, and if I suddenly discovered that the religious books read by me bore a different interpretation from the one I had learnt to give them, I should still hold to the view of Ahimsa as I am about to set forth here.

Our Shastras seem to teach that a man who really practises Ahimsa in its fullness has the world at his feet ; he so affects his surroundings that even the snakes and other venomous reptiles do him no harm. This is said to have been the experience of St. Francis of Assisi.

In its negative form it means not injuring any living being whether by body or mind. I may not, therefore, hurt the person of any wrong-doer or bear any ill-will to him and so cause him mental suffering. This statement does not cover suffering caused to the wrong-doer by natural acts of mine which do not proceed from ill-will. It, therefore, does not prevent me from withdrawing from his presence a child whom he, we shall imagine, is about to strike. Indeed, the proper practice of Ahimsa *requires* me to withdraw the intended victim from the wrong-doer, if I am in any way whatsoever the guardian of such a child. It was, therefore, most proper for the passive resisters of South Africa to have resisted the evil that the Union Government sought to do them. They bore no ill-will to it. They showed this by helping the Government whenever it needed their help. *Their resistance consisted of disobedience of the orders of the Government, even to the extent of suffering death at their hands.* Ahimsa requires deliberate self-suffering, not a deliberate injuring of the supposed wrong-doer.

In its positive form, Ahimsa means the largest love, the greatest charity. If I am a follower of Ahimsa, I *must love* my enemy. I must apply the same rules to the wrong-doer who is my enemy or a stranger to me, as I would to my wrong-doing father or son. This active Ahimsa necessarily includes truth and fearlessness. A man cannot deceive the loved one, he does not fear or frighten him or her. Gift of life is the greatest of all gifts.

A man who gives it in reality, disarms all hostility. He has paved the way for an honourable understanding. And none who is himself subject to fear can bestow that gift. He must, therefore, be himself fearless. A man cannot then practise Ahimsa and be a coward at the same time. The practice of Ahimsa calls forth the greatest courage. It is the most soldierly of soldier's virtues. General Gordon has been represented in a famous statue as bearing only a stick. This takes us far on the road to Ahimsa. But a soldier, who needs the protection of even a stick, is to that extent so much the less a soldier. He is the true soldier who knows how to die and stand his ground in the midst of a hail of bullets. Such a one was Ambarish, who stood his ground without lifting a finger though Durvasa did his worst. The Moors who were being pounded by the French gunners and who rushed to the guns' mouths with 'Allah' on their lips, showed much the same type of courage. Only theirs was the courage of desperation. Ambarisha's was due to love. Yet the Moorish valour, readiness to die, conquered the gunners. They frantically waved their hats, ceased firing, and greeted their erstwhile enemies as comrades. And so the South African passive resisters in their thousands were ready to die rather than sell their honour for a little personal ease. This was Ahimsa in its active form. It *never* barters away honour. A helpless girl in the hands of a follower of Ahimsa finds better and surer protection than in the hands of one who is prepared to defend her only to the point to which his weapons would carry him. The tyrant, in the first instance, will have to walk to his victim over the dead body of her defender; in the second, he has but to overpower the defender; for it is assumed that the canon of propriety in the second instance will be satisfied which the defender has fought to the extent of his physical valour. In the first instance, as the defender has matched his very soul against the mere body of the tyrant, the odds are that the soul in the latter will be awakened, and the girl would stand an infinitely greater chance of her honour being protected than in any other conceivable circumstance, barring, of course, that of her own personal courage.

If we are unmanly to-day, we are so, not because we do not know how to strike, but because we fear to die. He is no follower of Mahavira, the apostle of Jainism, or of Buddha or of the Vedas, who being afraid to die, takes flight before any danger, real or imaginary, all the while wishing that somebody else would remove the danger by destroying the person causing it. He is no follower of Ahimsa who does not care a straw if he kills a man by inches by deceiving him in trade, or who would protect by force of arms a few cows and make away with the butcher, or who, in order to do a supposed good to his country, does not mind killing off a few officials. All these are actuated by hatred, cowardice, and fear. Here love of the cow or the country is a vague thing intended to satisfy one's vanity or soothe a stinging conscience.

Ahimsa, truly understood, is, in my humble opinion, a panacea for all evils mundane and extra-mundane. We can never overdo it. Just at present we are not doing at all. Ahimsa does not displace the practice of other virtues, but renders their practice imperatively necessary before it can be practised even in its rudiments. Mahavira and Buddha were soldiers, and so was Tolstoy. Only they saw deeper and truer into their profession, and found the secret of a true, happy, honourable, and godly life. Let us be joint sharers with these teachers, and this land of ours will once more be the abode of Gods.—(*Modern Review*).

CIVIC FREEDOM

This is an incident that happened when he went to England:—

A gentleman on board said, "I see you are going to London in order to get rid of the day's collar!" Precisely; it was because they did not want to wear a dog's collar that they had put up that fight. They were willing to sacrifice everything for sentiment, but it was a noble sentiment. It was a sentiment that had to be cherished as a religious sentiment. It was a sentiment that bound people together; it was a sentiment that bound creatures to the Creator. That was the sentiment for which he asked them, advised them, if necessary, to die. Their action would be reflected throughout the British Dominions, through the length and breadth of India, and they were now upon their trial. There was no better and no fear for a man who believed in God. No matter what might be said, he would always repeat that it was a struggle for religious liberty. By religion they did not mean formal religion, or customary religion, but that religion which underlay all religions, which brought them face to face with their *Maker.* If they ceased to be men; if, on taking a deliberate vow, they broke that vow in order that they might remain in the Transvaal without physical inconvenience, they undoubtedly forsook their God. To repeat again the words of the Jew of Nazareth, those who would follow God had to leave the world, and he had called upon his countrymen, in that particular instance, to leave the world and cling to God, as a child would cling to the mother's breast.

Their natural deaths they could die far outside the Transvaal, wherever there was a piece of earth given them, but if they would die a noble death, a man's death, there was only one course open to them. . .

The handful of Indians who had a right to remain in the Transvaal should be allowed to remain as worthy citizens of a mighty Empire, but should not remain as beasts so long as he could help it.

WOMEN AND PASSIVE RESISTANCE

Conversation between Mr. and Mrs. Gandhi:—

The ladies were allowed to join the struggle after great effort was made by them to take part in it. When Mrs. Gandhi understood the marriage difficulty, she was incensed and said to Mr. Gandhi: "Then I am not your wife, according to the laws of this country." Mr. Gandhi replied that that was so and added that their children were not theirs. "Then" she said "let us go to India." Mr. Gandhi replied that that would be cowardly and that it would not solve the difficulty. "Could I not, then, join the struggle and be imprisoned myself?" Mr. Gandhi told her she could but that it was not a small matter. Her health was not good, she had not known that type of hardship and it would be disgraceful if, after her joining the struggle, she weakened. But Mrs. Gandhi was not to be moved. The other ladies, so closely related and living on the Settlement, would not be gainsaid. They insisted that, apart from their own convictions, just as strong as Mrs. Gandhi's, they could not possibly remain out and allow Mrs. Gandhi to go to gaol. The proposal caused the gravest anxiety. The step was momentous. If the decision was based on the impulse of the moment, they and those who allowed them to join might have to rue the day that it was made and accepted. Then how could they ensure being arrested without making a fuss? They wanted to avoid all publicity till they were safely in gaol. Then there was the risk of the Government leaving them alone as being harmless maniacs and fanatics. If, at the last moment, they flinched, their prominence might seriously damage the cause they sought to advance. All these and several other considerations suggested that the best course would be to diliberately and openly decline to disclose their identity on courting arrest. And if the move failed even then, they were to proceed to Johannesburg and take up hawking without licences and compel arrest. Any hardship was light enough compared to that of having to bear the insult to them or their sisters of not being considered lawful wives of their husbands.

APPENDIX III

APPRECIATIONS OF MR. GANDHI

By *Lord Ampthill*

Mr. Doke does not pretend to give more than a short biography and character sketch of Mr. Mohandas Karamchand Gandhi, the leader of the Indian community in Transvaal, but the importance of the book is due to the facts that men and matters are inseparably connected in all human affairs, and that the proper comprehension of political affairs in particular ever depends on a knowledge of the character and motives of those who direct them.

Although I am not in a position to criticise I do not doubt that in these pages the facts are accurately recorded, and I have sufficient reason to believe that the appreciation is just.

The subject of the sketch, Mr. Gandhi, has been denounced in this country, even by responsible persons, as an ordinary agitator; his acts have been misrepresented as mere vulgar defiance of the law; there have not been wanting suggestions that his motives are those of self-interest and pecuniary profit.

A perusal of these pages ought to dispel any such notions from the mind of any fair man who has been misled into entertaining them. And with a better knowledge of the man there must come a better knowledge of the matter.—(*Extract from the preface to Mr. Doke's book—Biography of Mr. Gandhi*).

By MRS. BESANT

Mr. Gandhi's birth-day was celebrated at the Gokhale's Hall, Madras, in Oct. 1917, *when Mrs. Besant before unveiling a portrait presented by Mr. G. A. Natesan spoke as follows:—*

FRIENDS,—If Mr. Gandhi had known that this gathering was to be held, he would have objected to it very strongly, but we have to think of the country and not of Mr. Gandhi alone. If Mr. Gandhi chooses to develop so noble a character as he has done, he no longer belongs to himself: he belongs to the Motherland (Cheers), and there is nothing more inspiring especially to the young, than to have held up before them the example of such a man. We cannot permit him to live in the obscurity that he loves. His deeds make a light around him, and if he tries to hide himself in the dark, he shines so brilliantly there that the darkness only increases the radiance of the light that he sheds. (Cheers.) Hence, we feel that whatever his personal ideas may be, India cannot spare him but must have him standing as an example of

MR. HAJEE HOOSEN DAVOOD
Who even on his death bed, was eager to suffer for the cause.

MRS. ANNIE BESANT,
One of the most ardent and eloquent advocate of fair and just treatment to Indians in South Africa.

an ideal Indian, for Mr. Gandhi represents in this country the highest ideal of a Sannyasi, a man who has renounced everything including himself and lives only for service. Two forces of service are recognised in the great faith to which Mr. Gandhi belongs; one is the service of a little developed man who serves in order to learn, to whom the duty of more developed people is that they should associate with him, that they should help him to educate himself, to help him to grow in strength, in purity and in knowledge. That is the service which is involuntary because practically compelled. Nature has not yet developed in such men the power to do aught save learn by service. Whatever body they may be born in, they are undeveloped in a true humanity of the spirit. Then as evolution proceeds and humanity rises from step to step, at last having acquired experience and courage and wisdom and will-power, the whole of these are gathered up into a man who is touching perfection, and then asking nothing more from the world, desiring nothing that the world can give, having learnt what the world has to teach, and needing nothing more, then he takes that highest service which is voluntary, which is gladly given which consecrates him to the service of humanity so long as there are any who need his help, so long as there are any whom he can lift nearer to his own position. That is the position of a Sannyasi—the servant of humanity—and it is that position in which Mr. Gandhi stands. It is the highest Hindu ideal, and he embodies it in himself and you will find that he has brought with him all the various virtues which mark the ascending marks of humanity. It is such a man that we honour here. He does not change, he does not actively oppose, but he sits as a rock. When that is the attitude of a man in connection with his dealings with the Government, the best thing that the Government does is to put him on a Committee. This is Mr. Gokhale's Hall, and it is but fitting that what Mr. Gokhale admired should be admired by all who are gathered here. (Cheers.)

By SIR P. M. MEHTA

Mr. Gandhi was a great believer in reason and in argument. He called him an unpractical man, and with all the admiration he had for Mr. Gandhi he disagreed with him on this point. He asked for too little (Laughter). If he had asked for the full rights of every Indian for access to the British dominions and had stuck to the full demand he might have got something. (Laughter). It was a great blunder, but it showed the reasonable character of the campaign led by Mr. Gandhi. He was again at the old game. What was the result? No one would listen to him, and still Indians in South Africa were asked to practice moderation!

By LADY MEHTA

In moving this Resolution I do not propose to refer to the serious developments that have arisen or to discuss the merits of the assertions and denials which have been made on either side, though it would not be difficult to point out that many of the denials contain in themselves admissions which it is difficult for us to contemplate without intense pain and anguish, I may be permitted however to say that it is impossible not to regret that there are people who in their wisdom have been lavish in advising the leaders of the Indian struggle in South Africa and their sorrowing and indignant sympathisers, in this country to exercise the virtue of moderation. Alas! It is a pity that these critics do not themselves practise the virtue which they unctuously preach, for if they to do so *they would realize that the constant words for years and years of the great noble and self sacrificing leader of the Indian struggle, Mr. Gandhi and his associates, have been unswerving loyalty on the one hand, and patience, resignation and above all moderation on the other. Moderation has been the guiding principle of Mr. Gandhi's gospel under the most trying circumstances.* The loyal, mild, patient and peace-abiding Indian subjects of our gracious Sovereign in South Africa have suffered humiliation and hardships for years hoping against hope believing in the justice and righteousness of their cause and confident in the ultimate protection of the Crown to which South Africans as well as ourselves owe submission and allegiance. They as well as we, could have claimed equal rights of entry and residence in any part of the dominions of our common Sovereign as guaranteed to us by solemn, charters. They as well, as we could have knocked at open doors in South Africa as well as Europeans have claimed to knock at open doors in all parts of Asia, indeed everywhere in the world. But so moderate have been Mr. Gandhi and his associates, that they bowed to the unrelenting fates and submitted practically and substantially to abandon all claims to free immigration. All that they asked for was that Indians already settled in South Africa should not be denied the bare rights which the simplest dignity of humanity required for free men and free citizens.

By MRS. SAROJINI NAIDU

Mrs. Sarojini Naidu has addressed the following letter to Lady Mehta :—

DEAR LADY MEHTA,—I venture to write to you as I see by the papers that you are the presiding genius of the forthcoming function to welcome my friend Mrs. Gandhi home again. I feel that though it may be the special privilege of the ladies of Bombay to accord her this personal ovation, all Indian women must desire to associate themselves with you in spirit to do honour to one who by her race, qualities of courage, devotion, and self-sacrifice has so signally justified and fulfilled the high traditions of Indian womanhood.

I believe I am one of the few people now back in India who had the good fortune to share the intimate homelife of Mr. and Mrs. Gandhi in England: and I cherish two or three memories of this brief period in connection with the kindly and gentle lady, whose name has become a household word in our midst with her broken health and her invincible fortitude—the fragile body of a child and the indomitable spirit of a martyr.

I recall my first meeting with them the day after their arrival in England. It was on a rainy August afternoon last year that I climbed the staircase of an ordinary London dwelling house to find myself confronted with a true Hindu idol of radiant and ascetic simplicity. The great South African leader who, to quote Mr. Gokhale's apt phrase, had moulded heroes out of clay, was reclining, a little ill and weary, on the floor eating his frugal meal of nuts and fruit (which I shared) and his wife was busy and content as though she were a mere modest housewife absorbed in a hundred details of household service, and not the world-famed heroine of a hundred noble sufferings in a nation's cause.

I recall too the brilliant and thrilling occasion

when men and women of all nationalities from East and West were gathered together to greet them in convincing proof that true greatness speaks with a universal tongue and compels a universal homage. She sat by her husband's side, simple and serene and dignified in the hour of triumph as she had proved herself simple and serene and dauntless in the hour of trial and tragedy.

I have a vision too of her brave, frail, pain worn hand must have held aloft the lamp of her country's honour undimmed in one alien land, working at rough garments for wounded soldiers in another . . . . Red Cross work.

But, there is one memory that to me is most precious and poignant, which I record as my personal tribute to her, and which serves not only to confirm but to complete and crown all the beautiful and lofty virtues that have made her an ideal comrade and helpmate to her husband. On her arrival in England in the early days of the war, one felt that Mrs. Gandhi was like a bird with eager outstretched wings longing to annihilate the time and distance that lay before her and her far-off India, and impatient of the brief and necessary interruption in her homeward flight. The woman's heart within her was full of yearning for the accustomed sounds and scenes of her own land and the mother's heart within her full of passionate hunger for the beloved faces of her children . . . . . And yet when her husband soon after, felt the call, strong and urgent to offer his services to the Empire and to form, the Ambulance Corps that has since done such splendid work, she reached the high watermark of her loyal devotion to him for she accepted his decision and strengthened his purpose with a prompt and willing renunciation of all her most dear and pressing desires. This to me is the real meaning of Sati. And it is this ready capacity for self-negation that has made me recognise anew that the true standard of a country's greatness lies not so much in its intellectual achievement and material prosperity as the undying spiritual ideals of love and service and sacrifice that inspire and sustain the mothers of the race.

I pray that the men of India may learn to realize in an increasing measure that it is through the worthiness of their lives and the nobility of their character alone that we women can hope to find the opportunity and inspiration to adequately fulfil the finest possibilities of our womanhood even as Mrs. Gandhi has fulfilled hers.

Believe me,

Yours sincerely,

(Sd.) SAROJINI NAIDU.

By MR. GOKHALE

.........Mr. Gandhi has not entered on the struggle without the fullest realisation of the situation and certainly he has not entered on it in light-hearted spirit. He knows that odds this time are tremendously against Indians. The Government will not yield if it can help it. The Imperial Government will be reluctant to exert any further pressure in favour of passive resistance and among Indians themselves already exhausted by the last struggle weakened persons will be found shrinking from sacrifices involved and advocating submission. But Mr. Gandhi is full of courage and what is more he is full of hope. He has planned his campaign carefully and whether he succeeds or fails he will push on like a hero to the end. The struggle this time, as I have already pointed out, is not confined to one province but extends to the whole of South Africa and not only men but women are taking part in it. From what I have seen of Mr. Gandhi's hold over our countrymen in South Africa, I have no doubt in my mind that thousands will be glad to suffer under his banner and his spirit will inspire them all. The last telegram which I had from him two days ago speaks in enthusiastic terms of bravery and heroism which women who are taking part in the struggle are showing. They are courting arrest. They put up with ill-treatment and even assaults without complaint and they are spreading the movement in all directions with wonderful zeal. The horrors of jail-life in South Africa with Kaffir warders devoid of all notions of humanity for Indian prisoners do not deter them and they are lifting the whole struggle to a plane which the last struggle even at its highest did not reach. Already two thousand families of indentured and exindentured men have joined the struggle. They are suspending work in collieries and on fields and unless Government guarantees repeal of £3 tax next season, industries which depend on Indian labour will soon be paralyzed and Government will have big job on its hands. Mr. Gandhi also went on to say that a growing minority of English is showing itself increasingly favourable to Indian demands and that the leaders of the Unionist party who did so much for us last session will, it is expected press Indian case with vigour when Parliament reassembles. But even if no assistance comes from any quarter, if the bulk of passive resisters retire from the struggle after enduring hardships for some time and if the prospect is altogether dark instead of being hopeful even then one hundred men and forty women are determined to perish in this struggle if need be rather than withdraw from it without achieving their object. They think that if everything else fails this supreme sacrifice on their part is necessary to prevent the Indian community in

South Africa from being crushed out of existence altogether. Do not let us be discouraged by a telegram which appeared the other day in papers about some Indians in Durban opposing this passive resistance movement and wanting to submit quietly to the indignities of the new position. When we think of suffering which will have to be endured and ruin that may have to be faced, is it any wonder knowing ourselves as we do that some Indians in South Africa should shrink from the ordeal? Is not the wonder rather this that so many men and women, Hindus, Mahomedans and Parsees, well-to-do and poor, should come forward to undergo sacrifice?

By BABU MOTILAL GHOSE

* * *

Be it borne in mind that the Indian labourers under the leadership of a saintly character like Mr. Gandhi and several other selfless and noble-hearted Indians and Europeans, are fighting not only for themselves but also for their motherland and the British Empire, nay, for humanity itself. Indeed the unparalleled spirit of self-sacrifice and heroic endurance they are displaying is bound to elevate the soul of every man who has a drop of humanity in him.

By THE HON. MOULVI A. K. FAZUL HAQUE

Extract from a speech at a protest meeting at the Calcutta Town Hall, said :—

* *

That this meeting accords its unqualified support to the passive resistance movement initiated by Indians for the redress of their grievances in South Africa and expresses its high sense of admiration for the heroism and self-sacrifice displayed by Mr. Gandhi and his followers and fellow-workers in carrying on this campaign against heavy odds.

He said there was no Indian whose sympathy did not go to the Indians in South Africa who were struggling, or the honor of their country. They in South Africa were forced to organise the passive resistance movement. Mr. Gandhi the organiser of the movement was its soul-force as it stood for higher to physical force and it was proper that they should record admiration for Mr. Gandhi.

MR. GANDHI IN LONDON

WELCOME RECEPTION AT THE HOTEL CECIL

A reception in honour of Mr. and Mrs. M. K. Gandhi and Mr. Kellenbach was held at the Hotel Cecil on Saturday afternoon (8th August 1914). About 150 persons attended, including Mr.

Bhupendranath Basu (Chairman of the Reception Committee) the Rt. Hon. Ameer Ali Singh, C. I. E., Mrs. Sarojini Naidu, Princes Sophia Duleep Singh, Lady Muir Meckenzie, Mrs. Despard, Mrs. Montefore, Lala Lajpat Rai, Hon. Mr. Krishna Sahay, Mr. M. A. Jinnah, Mr. S. Sinha, Mr. W. Douglashall, Mr. J. H. Polak, Colonel Varliker, Mr. F. H. Brown, Dr. J. N. Mehta, Mr. Fredrick Grubb, Mr. E. Dalgado, Mr. Syud Hussan, Dr. A. K. Kumaraswamy, Mr. Albert Cartwright, Mr. S. A. Bhisey, Mr. Zafar Ali Khan, Mr. M. M. Gandevia and Mr. S. Sorabji.

It was mentioned that letters of apology had been received from the Prime Minister, the Marquess of Crewe, K. G., Lord Curzon of Kedleston, Earl Roberts, Lord Ampthill, Lord Lamington, Lord Harris, the Hon. Mr. Gokhale, Mr. Ramsay MacDonald, M. P., Mr. Kier Hardie, M. P., and Mr. L. Harcourt, M. P.

Lord Gladstone wrote :—

" I much regret that my wife and I leave London to-morrow and cannot accept your courteous invitation to meet Mr. and Mrs. M. K. Gandhi and Mr. Kellenbach on Saturday. I much regret this, for the occasion will be a happy one as marking the settlement of outstanding British Indian grievances in South Africa in which your guests have taken so leading and so effective a part. Mr. Gandhi has shown a single-minded devotion to his cause which has won the admiration of all who understood the difficulty and danger of the position."

Mr. BHUPENDRANATH BASU

Mr. Bhupendranath Basu said that the Committee felt that, in spite of the great anxieties connected with the European situation, they could not let the occasion of Mr. and Mrs. Gandhi's visit to this country pass unnoticed. Mr. Gandhi's work in South Africa was known throughout the civilized world. His great devotion for principles won for him the affection of the fellow subjects, and had warm admiration from his strongest opponents. Mr. Gandhi's leadership had its strength in devotion to the sacred doctrine of returning love for hate. The Indians in South Africa had followed his leadership with absolute fidelity, being confident of his single-minded zeal for their cause. Mrs. Gandhi's conduct reminded him (Mr. Basu) of the spirit of the women of ancient India. Her work for the husband and for the cause he had taken up were worthy of the best traditions of their country's womanhood. Mr. Kallenbach, a stranger to them in race and creed, had suffered with them and for them, and his attachment for their cause would never be forgotten by a grateful people. With Indians working in Mr. Gandhi's spirit, they need never despair for the future of their country.

Mrs. SAROJINI NAIDU

Mrs. Sarojini Naidu said that the Indian people were under a deep debt of gratitude to Mr. Gandhi's work in South Africa for justice and truth had been a source of inspiration to the people of India; Olive Schreiner had described him as the Mazzini of the Indian movement in South Africa, and Mrs. Gandhi appealed to them as the ideal of wifehood and womanhood. On behalf of the company present, Mrs. Naidu then garlanded Mr. and Mrs. Gandhi and Mr. Kellenbach.

Mr. Gandhi's in reply said ;—

Mr. Gandhi, in returning thanks, referred to the great crisis which at the moment overshadowed the world. He hoped his young friends would "think Imperially" in the best sense of the word, and to their duty. With regard to affairs in South Africa, Mr. Gandhi paid a noble tribute to the devotion of his followers. It was to the rank and file that their victory was due. Those who had suffered and died in the struggle were the real heroes. He acknowledged the splendid help rendered by their fellow countrymen in India, especially that saintly politician Mr. Gokhale. Their noble Viceroy, Lord Hardinge had been a tower of strength to them. But their success would have been impossible had they not quickened the conscience of the people of South Africa by their passive resistance movement.

The masses of the people had given them splendid help throughout their march into the Transvaal. General Botha and his Government had also played the game, and General Smuts had been most anxious to do justice. Mr. Andrews had also played a noble part during his visit to South Africa last winter. Mr. Gandhi regarded the settlement as the Magna Charta of the South Africa British Indians, not because of the substance but because of the spirit which brought it about. There had been a change in the attitude of the people of South Africa and the settlement had been sealed by sufferings of the Indian community. It had proved that if Indians were in earnest they were irresistible. There had been no compromise in principles. Some grievances remained unredressed but these were capable of adjustment by pressure from Downing Street, Simla and from South Africa itself. The future rested upon themselves. If they proved worthy of better conditions, they would get them.

THE INDIAN FIELD AMBULANCE CORPS

AN APPEAL FOR MORE RECRUITS

To The Editor of "India."

Sir,

There were at Netley Hospital last Sunday nearly 470 Indian wounded soldiers. Many more are expected to arrive shortly, if they are not there already. The need for Indian-Volunteer orderlies is greater than ever. Nearly 70 members of the local Indian corps are already serving as nurses there. Leaving aside the medical members of the corps, there are now very few left to answer the further call when it comes.

May I therefore trespass upon the hospitality of your columns to appeal to the Indian young men residing in the United kingdom to enlist without delay? In my humble opinion it ought to be our proud privilege to nurse the Indian soldiers back to health. Colonel Bakers' cry is for more orderlies. And in order to make up the requisite number, as also to encourage our young men several elderly Indians occupying a high position have gone or are going to Netley as orderlies. Among them Mr. M. A. Turkhad, a former vice-president of the Rajkumar College in Kaithiawar, Mr. J. M. Parikh, Barrister-at-law, and Lieutenent Colonel Kanta Prasad of the Indian Medical service (Retired) who has served in five campaigns.

I hope that the example set by these gentlemen will inspire others with a like zeal, and that many Indians who can at all afford to do so will be equal to the emergency that has arisen. Those who desire to enlist can do so at tha Indian volunteer's committee's rooms at 16, Tribovir Road, near Earlls court, at any time during working hours.

M. K. GANDHI,

Chairman,

Indian Volunteers' Committee.

FAREWELL RECEPTION AT THE WESTMINISTER PALACE HOTEL

Mr. and Mrs. Gandhi who sailed for India on Saturday (Decr. 1914) were entertained by their friends on the previous afternoon at a farewell reception at the Westminister Palace Hotel. Mr. J. M. Parikh presided and among those present were Sir. Henry Cotton, Mr. Charles Roberts M. P. (Under Secretary of State for India) Mrs. Olive Schreiner, Sir Krishna Gupta, Mrs. Shuldam H. Shaw, Dr. J. C. Pollen, C. I. E., Mr. H. E. A. Cotton, L. C. C., Mr. and Mrs. N. C. Sen, Mr. and Mrs. J. H. Polak, Mr. A. Kallenbach, Lt. Col. Kanta Prasad I. M. S. (Retired) Miss F. Witerbottom, Dr. S. D. Bhabha, Dr. Jivraj N. Mehta, Mr. and Mrs. Basheshar Singh, Mr. and Mrs. Cheesman, Mr. F. N. Ilavna, Mr. E. Dalgado, Mr. Sorabji Shapurji and Mr. M. M. Gandevia.

Letters of apology for absence were announced from Sir William Wedderburn, Princess of Sophia Duleep Singh, the mambers of the Indian Ambulance corps at Netley, and Lt. Colonel. R. Baker, I. M. S. (commanding the corps), Mirza Abbas Baig Mr. and Mrs. Ratan J. Tata, Mr. C. E. Mallet, and Lt. Colonel and Mrs. Warliker.

SIR HENRY COTTON

Sir. Henry Cotton said that they had met that afternoon to give a cordial send-off to one who had earned by the labours and self-sacrifice over a very long period of years the esteem of every Englishman. It only remained for them to wish Mr. Gandhi a favourable journey to his native land and to congratulate him upon the triumphs he had achieved. Nor did they forget Mrs. Gandhi—hear, hear—who had also suffered in the good cause. Those labours and those sacrifices were over. Mr. Gandhi had practically won the battle he had been fighting and was returning to India to resume as they all hoped, the practice of his profession under happier auspices than it had been his fate to enjoy in South Africa, and to meet the thousands of his countrymen by whom his name would never be forgotten. (Cheers).

MR. PARIKH

Mr. J. M. Parikh added a few words on behalf of the Indians in London, both those who were permanent residents there and the young students whose stay was only brief. They had all had the great privilege of being closely associated with Mr. Gandhi during the past few weeks, and were well aware of the good work he had accomplished. Mr. Gandhi had not only thrown up a lucrative practice at the bar in South Africa in order to champion the cause of his countrymen, but together with his wife and his four sons had suffered imprisonment on a matter of principle. In London where he came in weak health, he had at once grasped the significance of the great crisis in which liberty and empire were alike involved. He immediately offered his services, and others had followed in his footsteps, with the result that the Field Ambulance corps had been established. Whatever had been the difficulties encountered, the success of the movement could be seen at Netley and Brighton, where youngmen of good family were cheerfully and willingly acting as hospital orderlies. (Hear, Hear).

MR. CHARLES ROBERTS, M.P.

Mr. Charles Roberts, M.P., said that the present was not the time for speeches, but they had met that afternoon to give expression in the most informal way to their personal feelings of good-will towards Mr. Gandhi and he was glad to contribute his share. The work which Mr. Gandhi had at heart was mainly accomplished as far as South Africa was concerned, although it might remain to be more completely fulfilled in other parts of the empire. He should like to take the opportunity to thank Mr. Gandhi for the help he had rendered to the Ambulance movement, and to testify to the really excellent work which Indians were doing in connection with it. (Hear Hear). It might be that in leaving England Mr. Gandhi felt to some extent disappointed of the hope of giving that help which he had so willingly afforded in South Africa ; but the prospect lay before him of more good work in India (Hear, Hear).

MRS. OLIVE SCHREINER

Mrs. Olive Schreiner expressed the great admiration which she felt for Mr. Gandhi. She looks upon him not only as the most able and self-sacrificing of leaders but also one of the teachers of the age who had given a high moral example to the world, and had striven for political justice and freedom, not by blood and violence but by the might force of passive resistance to what he believed to be Justice.

MR. GANDHI'S REPLY

Mr. Gandhi, who was received with cheers, said that his wife and himself were returning to the motherland with their work unaccomplished and with broken health, but he wished nevertheless, to use the language of hope. When the Ambulance corps was formed, it had been a matter of great joy to him that so many students and others came forward willingly and offered their services. Men such as Colonel Kanta prasad and Mr. Turkhud and Mr. Parikh were none of them expected to do the service of hospital orderlies at Netley, but nevertheless they had cheerfully done it. Indians had shown themselves thereby capable of doing their duty, if they received the recognition of their rights and privilegs. The whole idea of the corps arose because he felt that there should be some outlet for the anxiety of the Indians to help in the crisis which had come upon the Empire. (Hear, hear). He had himself pleaded hard with Mr. Roberts that some place should be found for him; but his health had not permitted and the doctors had been obdurate. He had not resigned from the corps. If in his own motherland he should be restored to strength, and hostilities were still continuing, he intended to come back, directly the summons reached him. (Cheers). As for his work in South Africa, they had been purely a matter of duty and carried no merit with it and his only aspiration on his return to his motherland was to do his duty as he found it day by day. He had been practically an exile for 25 years and his friend and master Mr. Gokhale had warned him not to speak of Indian questions, as India was a foreign land to him. (Laughter) But the India of his imagination was in India unrivalled in the world and India where the most spiritual treasures were to be found, and it was his dream and hope that the connection between India and England might be a source of spiritual comfort and uplifting to the whole world. He could not conclude without expressing his warmest appreciation of the great kindness which the Lady Cecilia Roberts had shown to his wife and himself in their illness. They had landed in England as strangers but they had speedily fallen among friends. There must be something good in the connection between India and England if it produces such unsolicitude and generous kindness from Englishmen and women to Indians.

LORD HARDINGE,
The Viceroy who won all hearts in India by his daring and patriotic Speech demanding Commission of inquiry in South Africa.

APPENDIX IV

LORD HARDINGE ON THE SOUTH AFRICAN SITUATION

In reply to the address presented by the Madras Mahajana Sabha on Monday *the 24th November* 1913, *His Excellency the Viceroy spoke as follows* :—

The position of Indians in South Africa has for some years past received the most anxious consideration of the Government of India, and, as the Mahajana Sabha acknowledge, they are doing all that lies in their power to ensure fair treatment for Indians residing within the Union.

The Act, of which you complain, has in practice the effect of putting a stop to Asiatic emigration to South Africa, though it does not discriminate in so many words against Asiatics. We have, however, succeeded in securing the privilege of entry for a limited number of educated Indians annually. We have also made special endeavours to secure as favourable terms as possible for Indians already resident in the Union, and our efforts have resulted in the inclusion of provisions for the right of appeal to the Courts on points of law, and of a definition of domicile, in accordance with which the position of

Indians, who entered the Union otherwise than under indenture, has been satisfactorily laid down.

We are at the present moment in communication with the Secretary of State regarding other restrictions contained in the Act to which we take exception and we trust that our representations may not be without result.

You have urged in your address that retaliatory measures should be taken by the Government of India but you have not attempted to state the particular measures which in your opinion should be adopted. As you are aware we forbade indentured emigration to Natal in 1911 : and the fact that the Natal planters sent a delegate over to India, to beg for a reconsideration of that measure shows how hardly it hit them. But I am afraid it has had but little effect upon South Africa as a whole, and it is unfortunately not easy to find means by which India can make her indignation seriously felt by those who hold the reins of Government in that country.

Recently, your compatriats in South Africa have taken matters into their own hands by organising what is called passive resistance to laws which they consider invidious and unjust—an opinion which we who watch their struggles from afar cannot but share.

They have violated as they intended to violate, those laws, with full knowledge of the penalties involved, and ready with all courage and patience to endure those penalties. In all this they have the sympathy of India—deep and burning—and not only of India, but of all those who like myself, without being Indians themselves, have feelings of sympathy for the people of this country.

But the most recent developments have taken a very serious turn and we have seen the widest publicity given to allegations that this movement of passive resistance has been dealt with by measures which would not for a moment be tolerated in any country that claims to call itself civilised.

These allegations have been met by a categorical denial from the responsible Government of South Africa, though even their denial contains admissions which do not seem to me to indicate that the Union Government have exercised a very wise discretion in some of the steps which they have adopted. That is the position at this moment, and I do feel that if the South African Government desire to justify themselves in the eyes of India and the world only one course is open to them and that is to appoint a strong and impartial committee, upon which Indian interests shall be fully represented, to conduct a thorough and searching enquiry into the truth of these allegations; and as the communique that has appeared in this morning's papers will show you, I have not hesitated to press that view upon the Secretary of State. Now that, according to telegraphic accounts received in this country from South Africa, such disorder as arose has completely ceased, I trust that the Government of the Union will fully realise the imperative necessity of treating a loyal section of their fellow subjects in a spirit of equity and in accordance with their rights as free citizens of the British Empire. You may rest assured that the Government of India will not cease to urge these considerations upon His Majesty's Government.

THE LORD BISHOP OF MADRAS ON THE SOUTH AFRICAN SITUATION

Under the auspices of the Indian South African League, a public meeting was held on the 15*th December* 1913 *in the Y.M.C.A. Auditorium to thank H.E. the Viceroy for his sympathetic assurances about the conditions of Indians in South Africa and to protest against the composition of the Committee appointed by the South African Union Government to go into the question. The Rev. Lord Bishop of Madras, the Chairman, said:—*

Gentlemen,—The object of this meeting is: to convey most respectfully our thanks to His Excellency the Viceroy for his remarks on the South African question during his recent visit to Madras, and our hearty appreciation of the deep sympathy which he has shown with the wrongs and sufferings of the Indians in South Africa and the wise and statesmanlike spirit in which he has dealt with this most painful and difficult question. I will leave the three speakers, who will respectively move, second and support the resolution that will be submitted to this meeting, to express your views on this subject, and also the gratitude which all classes of Indians in Madras feel towards His Excellency for his courageous and timely utterances. But before calling upon them to speak, I should like to say a few words as an Englishman and a Christian. I do not propose to argue all over, again the Indian question in South Africa except to emphasise once more the fact that Indians are not now claiming the free right of entry for the people of India to South Africa or any other part of the British Empire. What they do claim is that the Indians who have been allowed to settle in South Africa and make South Africa their home, the men and women by whose labour and toil Natal has been saved from ruin and made a prosperous colony, should be treated with common justice and humanity. If you have not done so already, I should advise you to procure and read carefully a copy of Mr. Gokhale's speech at Bombay on the 24th October last. It gives the clearest and fullest statement of the history of this struggle and of the Indian demands that I have read anywhere. I have nothing to add to what Mr.

Gokhale has already said so eloquently and so feelingly and yet with admirable self-restraint. But I will say just a few words on some of the criticisms which have been levelled against His Excellency the Viceroy in England and in South Africa.

UNDIPLOMATIC

In the first place his speech has been condemned as undiplomatic. Possibly it was undiplomatic. But there is a time for all things. For many years the Government of India have tried patiently to secure justice for the Indians in South Africa by diplomatic methods and they have failed. And now that matters have been brought to a dangerous crisis and all India is ablaze with a fiery indignation, time has come to put aside the soft phrases of diplomacy, to call a spade a spade and to tell the politicians of South Africa plainly how their action in this matter is regarded in India. We are deeply grateful to His Excellency that he has done this and has come forward at a critical time as the spokesman and representative of the Indian people.

Then, in the second place, His Excellency has been criticised for having, encouraged the men who are breaking the law. No sensible person would ever say a word to encourage law-breaking without a deep sense or responsibility. It is a platitude to say that society is built up on respect for law and order. But there is such a thing as tyranny masquerading under the forms of law; and when that is unhappily the case, resistance to law becomes not a crime, but a virtue. I shirnk from saying anything that may even seem to encourage lawlessness; but I think that it is necessary to say quite plainly and openly that the Indians in South Africa are now resisting not law but tyranny. They have been very patient. For twenty years or more they have pleaded for justice, and it is only after exhausting every other possible means of securing redress for their cruel wrongs, that they have at last taken the step of passive resistance to unjust laws. For the South African Government, therefore, to appeal to the duty of obedience to the law seems to me to ignore the obvious fact that the just complaints of the Indians for the last twenty years has been that the law has been made an engine of tyranny and injustice. It is all very well for the South African Government to say, 'we cannot consider your grievances till you cease your resistance to the law.' The Indians can say with far more reason: 'we will cease our resistance to your laws when you cease to make them Instruments of oppression.' In saying this, I do not for a moment condone any acts of unprovoked violence that may have occurred on the part of the Indians; I must repeat with regard to these outbreaks what I have already said elsewhere, that the responsibility for them must rest mainly upon those who have provoked the conflict by injustice and cruelty.

I have spoken so far as an Englishmen, taught from my childhood to hate tyranny and to regard it as a sacred duty to stand up for the oppressed and persecuted, to whatever race or country they belong. May I say just a very few words as a Christian. I feel all the more indignant at the cruel injustice inflicted on the Indians in South Africa just because it is inflicted by men who profess to be disciples and followers of Jesus Christ. Tyranny is hateful in any case. It is doubly hateful when exercised by Christians in direct defiance of their creed and in flagrant opposition to the whole teaching and example of Him whom they acknowledge as their Lord and their God. I frankly confess, though it deeply grieves me to say it, that I see in Mr. Gandhi the patient sufferer for the cause of righteousness and mercy, a truer representative of the Crucified Saviour than the men who have thrown him into prison and yet call themselves by the name of Christ.

COUNT L. N. TOLSTOY,

The great Russian Passive Resister, who addressed a letter to Mr. Gandhi.

SIR RABINDRANATH TAGORE,

"The power our fellow-countrymen have shown in standing firm for their cause under severest trials, fighting unarmed against fearful odds, has given us, a firmer faith in the strength of the God that can defy sufferings and defeats at the hands of physical supremacy, that can make its gains of its losses."

APPENDIX V

TOLSTOY ON PASSIVE RESISTANCE

The following is a translation of the letter of *Count Tolstoy* to Mr. Gandhi :—

Kotchety, Russia, Sept. 7, 1910.

I received your journal, and was pleased to learn all contained therein concerning the passive resisters. And I felt like telling you all the thoughts which that reading called up in me.

The longer I live, and especially now, when I vividly feel the nearness of death, I want to tell others what I feel so particularly, clearly and what to my mind is of great importance—namely, that which is called passive resistance, but which is in reality nothing else than the teaching of love uncorrupted by false interpretations. That love—i.e., the striving for the union of human souls and the activity derived from this striving—is the highest and only law of human life, and in the depth of his soul every human being (as we most clearly see in children) feels and knows this; he knows this until he is entangled by the false teachings of the world. This law was proclaimed by all—by the Indian as by the Chinese, Hebrew,

Greek and Roman sages of the world. I think this law was most clearly expressed by Christ, who plainly said that "in this only is all the law and the prophets." But besides this, foreseeing the corruption to which this law is and may be subject, he straightway pointed out the danger of its corruption, which is natural to people who live in worldly interests, the danger, namely, which justifies the defence of these interests by the use of force, or, as he said, "with blows to answer blows, by force to take back things usurped," etc. He knew, as every sensible man must know, that the use of force is incompatible with love as the fundamental law of life, that as soon as violence is permitted, in whichever case it may be, the insufficiency of the law of love is acknowledged, and by this the very law is denied. The whole Christian civilisation, so brilliant outwardly, grew upon this self-evident and strange misunderstanding and contradiction, sometimes conscious, but mostly unconscious.

In reality, as soon as force was admitted into love there was no more, and there could be no love as the law of life, and as there was no law of love, there was no law at all, except violence—*i.e.*, the power of the strongest. So lived Christian humanity for nineteen centuries. It is true that in all times people were guided by violence in arranging their lives. The difference between the Christian nations and all other nations is only that in the Christian world the law of love was expressed clearly and definitely, whereas it was not so expressed in any other religious teaching, and that the people of the Christian world have solemnly accepted this law, whilst at the same time they have permitted violence, and built their lives on violence, and that is why the whole life of the Christian peoples is a continuous contradiction between that which they profess and the principles on which they order their lives—a contradiction between love accepted as the law of life and violence which is recognised and praised, acknowledged even as a necessity in different phases of life, such as the power of rulers, courts and armies. This contradiction always grew with the development of the people of the Christian world, and lately it reached the highest stage. The question now evidently stands thus: either to admit that we do not recognise any religio-moral teaching, and we guide ourselves in arranging our lives only by power of the stronger, or that all our compulsory taxes, court and police establishments, but mainly our armies, must be abolished.

This year, in Spring, at a Scripture examination in a girls' high school at Moscow, the teacher and the bishop present asked the girls questions on the Commandments, and especially on the sixth. After a correct answer, the bishop generally put another question, whether murder was always in all cases forbidden by God's law, and the unhappy young ladies were forced by previous instruction to answer, "Not always"—that murder was permitted in war and in execution of criminals. Still, when one of these unfortunate young ladies (what I am telling is not an invention, but a fact told me by an eye-witness), after her first answer, was asked the usual question, if killing were always sinful, she, agitated and blushing, decisively answered, "Always," and to all the usual sophisms of the bishop she answered with decided conviction, that killing always was forbidden in the Old Testament and forbidden by Christ, not only killing, but even every wrong against a brother. Notwithstanding all his grandeur and art of speech, the bishop became silent and the girl remained victorious.

Yes, we can talk in our newspapers of the progress of aviation, of complicated diplomatic relations, of different clubs and conventions, of unions of different kinds, of so-called productions of art, and keep silent about what that young lady said. But it cannot be passed over in silence, because it is felt, more or less dimly, but always felt by every man in the Christian world. Socialism Communism, Anarchism, Salvation Army, increasing crime, unemployment, the growing insane luxury of the rich and misery of the poor, the alarmingly increasing number of suicides—all these are the signs of that internal contradiction which must be solved and cannot remain unsolved. And of course solved in the sense of acknowledging the law of love and denying violence. *And so your activity in the Transvaal, as it seems to us, at the end of the world, is the most essential work, the most important of all the work now being done in the world, and in which not only the nations of the Christian, but of all the world, will unavoidably take part.*

I think that you will be pleased to know that here in Russia this activity is also fast developing in the way of refusals to serve in the Army, the number of which increases from year to year. However insignificant is the number of our people who are passive resisters in Russia who refuse to serve in the Army, these and the others can boldly say that God is with them. And God is more powerful than man.

In acknowledging Christianity even in that corrupt form in which it is professed amongst the Christian nations, and at the same time in acknowledging the necessity of armies and armament for killing on the greatest scale in wars, there is such a clear clamouring contradiction, that it must sooner or later, possibly very soon, inevitably reveal itself and annihilate either the professing of the Christian religion, which is indispensable in keeping up these forces, or the existence of armies and all the violence kept up by them, which is not less necessary for power. This contradiction is felt by all government, by your British as well as by our Russian Government, and out of a general feeling of self-preservation the persecution by them (as seen in Russia and in the journal sent by you) against such anti-government activity as those above-mentioned, is carried on with more energy than against any other form of opposition. The governments know where their chief danger lies, and they vigilantly guard in this question, not only their interests, but the question: "To be or not to be?"—

Yours very faithfully,

LEO TOLSTOY.

[Translated from the original Russian by Pauline Padlashuk.—Johannesburg, November 15, 1910.]

Indian Opinion.

APPENDIX VI

INDIGO LABOUR IN BEHAR

MR. GANDHI AT MOTIHARI

MAGISTRATES ORDER

Mr. Gandhi left Muzaffarpur for Motihari by the mid-day train on the 15th April 1917. Next day he was served with a notice under Sec. 144 Cr. P. Code, of which the following is a copy.

Mr. M. K. Gandhi, at present in Motihari.

Whereas it has been made to appear to me from the letter of the commissioner of the Division copy of which is attached to this order, that your presence in any part of the district will endanger the public peace, and may lead to serious disturbance which may be accompanied by loss of life, and whereas urgency is of the utmost importance.

Now, therefore, I do hereby order you to abstain from remaining in this district, which you are required to leave by the next available train.

(Sd.) W. B. HEYCOCK,

16th April, 1917. *District Magistrate,*

Champaran.

WHAT THE COMMISSIONER THOUGHT

Copy of the letter from the Commissioner, Tirhut Division, to the District Magistrate of Champaran, dated Muzaffarpur, the 13th April, 1917 :

Sir,

Mr. M. K. Gandhi has come here in response to what he describes as an insistent public demand, to inquire into the conditions under which Indians work on indigo plantations, and desires the help of the local administration. He came to see me this morning ; and I explained that relations between the planters and raiyats had engaged the attention of the administration since the sixties, and that we were particularly concerned with a phase of the problem in Champaran now ; but it was doubtful whether the intervention of a stranger in the middle of our treatment of the case would not prove an embarrassment. I indicated the potentialities of disturbance in Champaran, asked for credentials to show an insistent public demand for his enquiry, and said that the matter would probably need reference to Government.

I expect that Mr. Gandhi will communicate with me again before he proceeds to Champaran, but have been informed since our interview that his object is likely to be agitation, rather than a genuine search for knowledge, and it is possible that he may proceed without further reference. I consider that there is a danger of disturbance to the public tranquillity, should he visit your district; and I have the honour to request you to direct him by an order under Sec. 144, Cr. P. C., to leave at once, if he should appear.

I have the honour to be, etc.,

(Sd.) L. F. MORSHEAD,

Commissioner of Tirhut Division.

MR. GANDHI'S REPLY

Mr. Gandhi's reply to the District Magistrate, Motihari:

Sir,—With reference to the order under Sec. 144, Cr. P. C., just served upon me, I beg to state that I am sorry that you have felt called upon to issue it; and I am sorry too that the Commissioner of the Division has totally misinterpreted my position. Out of a sense of public responsibility, I feel it to be my duty to say that I am unable to leave this district, but if it so pleases the authorities, I shall submit to the order by suffering the penalty of disobedience.

I most emphatically repudiate the Commissioner's suggestion that "my object is likely to be agitation." My desire is purely and simply for

" a genuine search for knowledge " and this I shall continue to satisfy so long as I am left free.

I have, etc.,

16th April, 1917. (Sd.) M. K. GANDHI.

IN COURT

Mr. Gandhi appeared before the Deputy Magistrate on Wednesday, the 18th instant. He read the Statement printed below, and being asked to plead and finding that the case was likely to be unnecessarily prolonged, pleaded guilty. The Magistrate would not award the penalty but postponed judgment till 3 P.M. Meanwhile, he was asked to see the Superintendent and then the District Magistrate. The result was that he agreed not to go out to the villages pending instructions from the Government as to their view of his mission. The case was then postponed up to Saturday, April 21.

MR. GANDHI'S STATEMENT

The following is the text of Mr. Gandhi's Statement before the Court :

With the permission of the Court, I would like to make a brief statement showing why I have taken the very serious step of seemingly disobeying the order made under Sec. 144 of the Cr. P. C. In my humble opinion, it is a question of difference of opinion, between the local administration and myself. I have entered the country with motives of rendering humanitarian and national service. I have done so in response to a pressing invitation to come and help the raiyats, who urge they are not being fairly treated by the indigo planters. I could not render any help without studying the problem. I have therefore, come to study it with the assistance, if possible of the administration and the planters. I have no other motive, and I cannot believe that my coming here can in any way disturb public peace or cause loss of life. I claim to have considerable experience in such matters. The administration, however, have thought differently. I fully appreciate their difficulty, and I admit too, that they can only proceed upon information they receive. As a law-abiding citizen, my first instinct would be as it was to obey the order served upon me. I could not do so without doing violence to my sense of duty to those for whom I came. I feel that I could just now serve them only by remaining in their midst. I could not, therefore, voluntarily retire. Amid this conflict of duty, I could only throw the responsibility of removing me from them on the administration. I am fully conscious of the fact that a person, holding in the public life of India a position such as I do, has to be most careful in setting examples. It is my firm belief that, in the complex constitution under which we are living, the safe and honourable course for a self respecting man is, in the circumstances such as that face me, to do what I have decided to do, that is, to submit without protest to the penalty of disobedience. I have ventured to make this statement not in any way in extenuation of the penalty to be awarded against me, but to show that I have disregarded the order served upon me, not for want of respect for lawful authority, but in obedience to the higher law of our being—the voice of conscience.—*Leader.*

Government Committee of Enquiry

MR. M. K. GANDHI TO SIT AS MEMBER

Bankipore, June 1917 :—

The Local Government have to-day issued a resolution regarding the appintment of a committee to enquire into the relations between landlord and tenant in the Champaran district, including all disputes arising out of the manufacture and cultivation of indigo. The committee, as was stated in a previous message, is fully representative, appointed with the approval of the Government of India and consists of the following ;—President : Mr. F. G. Sly, Commissioner, Central Provinces ; Members : Mr. L. G. Adami, Legal Remembrancer, Behar and Orissa, the Hon. Raja Harihar Prashad Narayan Singh, a landlord, the Hon. Mr. D. J. Reicl a member of the planting community, Mr. G. Rainy, Deputy Secretary, Finance Department, Government of India, who had been in the Champaran District formerly and Mr. M. K. Gandhi, Secretary : Mr. E. L. Tanner, Settlement Officer, South Bihar. Mr. Tanner, it may be stated, was the Sub-Divisional Officer of Bettiah, when indigo riots broke out in that sub-division in 1908.

The committee's duty will also be to examine the evidence on those subjects already available, supplementing it by such further enquiry, local and otherwise, as they may consider desirable, and to report their conclusions to the Government, stating the measures they recommend in order to remove any abuse or grievances, which they may find to exist. The Lieut-Governor in Council has left a free hand to the Committee as to the procedure they will adopt in arriving at the facts. The committee will assemble about the 15th July, and will, it is hoped, complete their labours within three months.

Government Resolution

The resolution, appointing this Committee, says :— On various occasions during the past fifty years, the relations of landlords and tenants and the circumstances, attending the growing of indigo in the Champaran District, have been the cause of considerable anxiety. The conditions under which indigo was cultivated when the industry was flourishing, required readjustment when it declined simultaneously with a general rise in the prices of food grains, and it was partly on this account and partly owing to other local causes that disturbances broke out in certain indigo concerns in 1908. Mr. Gourlay was deputed by the Government of Bengal to investigate the causes of the disturbances, and his report and recommendations were considered at a series of conferences presided over by Sir Edward Baker, and attended by the local officers of the Government and representatives of the Behar Planters' Association. As a result of these discussions, revised conditions for the cultivation of indigo, calculated to remove the grievances of the raiyats, were accepted by the Behar Planters Association. In 1912 fresh agitation arose connected not so much with the conditions under which indigo was grown as with the action of certain factories, which were reducing their indigo manufacture, and taking agreements from their tenants for the payment, in lieu of indigo cultivation, of a lump sum in temporarily leased villages or of an increase of rent in villages under permanent lease. Numerous petitions on this subject were presented from time to time to the local officers and to Government, and petitions were at the same time field by raiyats of the villages in the north of the Bettiah sub-division, in which indigo had never been grown, complaining of the levy of abab or illegal additions to rent by their leaseholders, both Indian and European. The issues raised by all these petitions related primarily to rent and tenancy conditions, and as the revision settlement of the district was about to be undertaken, in the course of which the relations existing between landlords and tenants would come under detailed examination, it was thought advisable to await the report of the Settlement Officers before passing final orders on the petitions. The revision settlement was started in the cold weather of 1913. On the 7th April 1915 a resolution was moved in the Local Legislative Council asking for the appointment of a mixed committee of officials and non-officials to enquire into the complaints of the raiyat and to suggest remedies. It was negatived by a large majority including 12 out of the 16 non-official members of Council present on the ground that the appointment of such a committee at that stage was unnecessary, as the settlement officers were engaged in the collection of all the material required for the decision of the questions at issue, and an additional enquiry of the nature proposed would merely have the effect of further exaggerating the relations of landlord and tenant, which were already feeling the strain of the settlement operations. The settlement operations have now been completed in the northern portion of the district, and are approaching completion in the remainder, and a mass of evidence regarding agricultural conditions and the relations between landlords and tenants has been collected. A preliminary report on the complaints of the tenants in the leased villages in the north of the Bettiah sub-division, in which no indigo is grown, has been received, and action has already been taken to prohibit the levy of illegal cesses, and, in the case of the Bettiah Raj, to review the terms of the leases on which the villages concerned are held. As regards the complaints of the raiyats in other parts of the district, the final report of the Settlement Officer has not yet been received, but recent events have again brought into prominence the whole question of the relations between landlords and tenants and in particular the taking of agreements from the raiyats for compensation or for enhanced rent in return for the abandonment of indigo cultivation. In these circumstances and in deference to representations which have been received from various quarters that the time has come when an enquiry by a joint body of officials and non-officials might materially assist the Local Government in coming to a decision on the problems, which have arisen, the Lieut.-Governor in Council has decided, without waiting for the final report of the Settlement operations, to refer the question at issue to a committee of enquiry on which all interests concerned will be represented.

INDEX.

PAGE

N

O

T